BABYMAMAMANIA

*[bey-bee-mah-muh-**mey**-nee-uh]* - (**noun**)

A Social Study and Gospel Stage Play
by

Pastor Jenn

~ *Dedication* ~

What lies behind us and what lies before us
are small matters compared to what lies within us.
Resolve to succeed.
The greatest discovery one can make is
that nothing is impossible.
The harder the conflict,
the more glorious the triumph.

My sister is truly blessed with the God-given
talent to embrace and overcome all
challenges placed in front of her.
Job well done Jennifer,
I love you infinity!

James E. Gregory

~ Foreword ~

With my attention fixed to the television set like the crackhead to that allusive white speck on a beige carpet, I admit that I particularly look forward to my weekly intake of the Maury Show and his relentless aid in the search for confused women's baby daddies. For some reason, I am intrigued by the show's revelations as to who really is the "daddy" while Maury wages his never-ending saga into the lives of the many women unsure of the linage of their own children. Perhaps it's the shock element when I side with the T.V. audience concerning the atrocious actions of the baby daddy's denial of paternity, only to learn he really was telling the truth. I must confess that I will also even go as far as to close my eyes and plug my ears during the commercials that reveal the upcoming disclosures- I really do like being stunned by the findings within the infamous golden envelope.

Following many months spent researching the Maury Show on both the television and YouTube for my play *"Babymamamania"*, I have concluded there are two types of women generally represented on his program….it's either the hysterically crying baby mama- her seemingly forced tears streaming down as they make their indelible trail through all the foundation and blush. Or the other babymama is the angry one - always ready to rumble and quick to run over to the photos in an attempt to prove the child and the baby daddy have the same nose, the same ears etc, etc. Whichever one shows up each and every Monday, I cross my fingers…. I hold my breath….. I pray that their search will end today!

Regrettably while submerged in "my fix", I began to find myself less entertained and more dismayed by the antics of these women who actually *need* help in establishing paternity. Worse is the same woman returning time after time, testing man after man and is still unsuccessful in designating one of them as the father of her child. **Why Ladies… Why?** Even more targeted to the population I wish to address in this matter- **Why Sista's….Why**? Black people have spent much effort overcoming more than four centuries of injustices and degradation within our own country.

So to watch our younger generations feed into ageless stereotypes, bearing all on national television is definitely a thorn-in-the-side to most African-Americans that watch and shake their heads in disappointment. You can imagine my own disenchantment with this show as I witnessed a particular young Black woman run from Maury's stage in tears because **NONE** of the 16 men tested – *all 16 men she slept with at the same party; all 16 pictures of these young Black men unclothed before the national public* – not one was proved to be the father of her child! Two issues became clear to me as this dejected young woman bared her soul before all watching. First, it was evident that there are certainly deep emotional issues she must address as to why she would even allow herself to be in such an unconscionable state to sleep with so many men at one time. Secondly, Black America *must* address the social implications as to why our young Black men used her like that. To my dismay, I learned this was an update show and she had returned for the second visit to test the 17th man from the party *(she also had sex with this man again on the night* *following the infamous event)*. When it was proven he was not the father either, this prompted me to think about what does Maury actively do to help stem the tide of babies born out-of wedlock beyond his show's constant exposure of the dilemma. We know Maury to offer rehabilitation assistance to pregnant drug addict, boot-camp intervention to the out-of-control teen girl that beats her mother and on-set therapy for the man that treats his wife like his slave. Conversely, I have never seen any counselors making their way backstage to help the fallen babymama nor is there any advice, direction or guidance from Maury's resident psychotherapist Dr. Jeffrey to the baby mama to help her stop the destructive behavior. Even after a guest's disclosure shocked Maury into remarking "What the heck is going wrong in our country!" as usual, his only offer of help to the baby mama was to come back and test more men.

Look, I understand better than most how poor choices are made in the heat of passion whereby unplanned pregnancies can and often do occur- *been there…done that!* Yet I was astounded to learn that according to the American Pregnancy Association, of the 42 million sexually active women of child-bearing age in the United States, 3 million use **<u>NO</u>** contraception at all. Notwithstanding the physical dangers directly associated with such behavior, most troubling is the fact this small group of women actually account for **47% of all unplanned pregnancies in our county!** In plain English... **6% of all sexually active women between the ages of 15-44 are responsible for almost half of all unplanned pregnancies in this nation!** This is very sad... Something *–or even better-* someone has got to change!

Babymamamania

Table of Contents

The Definition

Babymamamania
[bey-bee-mah-m*uh*-**mey**-nee-*uh*]

Noun- (Origin: 2009; from Jennifer Gregory) derived from **baby mama** - _(Origin: 1966; from Jamaican Creole)_- a mother who is not married to or living with her child's father and **mania** - _(Origin: 1350–1400; from Greek mania-madness)_ a frenzied, out-of-control and widespread trend.

Definition: 1. A sweeping craze whereby women who have babies out-of-wedlock, psychologically impose upon the biological father to care for a child he had no intention of fathering and/or does not want to financially support.

Definition: 2. The belief in the absurd notion if a man has sex with a woman, he must want her to be his baby mama. If not, he would have used protection.

Definition: 3. The widespread fallacy that if a man continues to have sex on a regular basis with his baby mama, he must still have feelings for her.

Definition: 4. The pop-culture trend of baby mamas referring to the child's father as a fiancé when there is neither engagement ring nor commitment in sight.

The *Oxford English Dictionary* defines **baby mama** as "the mother of a man's child, who is not his wife or (in most cases) his current or exclusive partner." This term actually originated in Jamaican Creole as "**baby-mother**" (pronounced [bebi mada]), with the first printed usage appearing in the Kingston newspaper, *The Daily Gleaner* in 1966. Initially, the term was used by the fathers of children born out of wedlock to describe the mothers of their children, but now is generally used to describe any single mother. Later, as we have noticed the title becoming more familiar, baby mama terminology forever entered into our pop-culture primarily due to American hip-hop lyrics following the mid-1990s. Here's a few of the most well known examples:

> The *Outkast* song "Ms. Jackson", released in 2000, was dedicated to "all the baby mamas' mamas".

> *American Idol* winner Fantasia Barrino released a song entitled "Baby Mama" in 2004, and

13

Planet Earth, an album by Prince released in 2007, features a song called "Future Baby Mama".

More to the point however for the purpose of this writing, are the findings of Peter L. Patrick, a linguistics professor who studies Jamaican English. He has said this of the terms *baby mother* and *baby father:* "[they] definitely imply there is not a marriage—not even a common-law marriage, but rather that the child is an **'outside'** child". These children are conceived under such circumstances ranging anywhere from a one-night-stand to the consistent booty-call. While both the "baby mama" title *and* persona have been established with definite staying power, it is imperative that we as a nation begin to address the overwhelming ramifications that are directly associated with the stigma of unwed pregnancy going from shameful to celebratory in almost a single generation. The resulting children are now no longer labeled as "bastards" while unwed mothers are now openly embraced instead of shunned as had been the case in our country's past. Gone forever are the days of humiliation for the family for such indiscretions, especially when the baby mama happens to be famous. I believe that the media's constant and increasing glamorization of the "Brangelinas" of our country has indeed served as the major catalyst for the nation's recent tolerance and subsequent accommodation of fornication and the babies that are produced as an acceptable behavior. Just this week, *OK*'s cover featured the confirmed pregnant Jennifer Aniston along side Gerard Butler. The headline read "finally" a baby for Jen, as if all her fornication "finally" paid off and called Gerard "the bad boy to make her dream come true…. Wow, *OK* magazine actually congratulated the famous fornicators!

It is my contention that as we identify the *psychological* reasons why women willingly give themselves sexually to men who are not their husbands, we will unearth the obscurities that veil the true place of healing- a relationship with Jesus the Christ. Only then can we find the power to curb the self-destructive sexual behaviors, slow the tidal wave of out-of-wedlock pregnancies, and "finally" put the mystique and allure of even wanting to be a baby mama to rest.

The Truth

Unless a woman is forced to have unprotected premarital sex, all negative experiences resulting from being a baby mama is entirely her fault.

Pastor Jenn

The very complexity surrounding why women make the decision to have premarital, unprotected sex unquestionably rests within a myriad of reasons ranging from self-esteem issues to those of deep lusts. Ultimately, the decision regarding when to have consensual sex does rest solely with the woman, however the motives behind these life-altering choices are as vast as the population doing the deed. If we are truly honest with ourselves, from within a warped psyche formed by dark points in our past, women have

16

even used sex as a numbing salve to sooth the wounded heart or as replacement for what was recently lost. I know this for myself. Let me keep it R.E.A.L.- I am preaching to the choir.

Whether the woman is needy or just naughty, there are definitely personal and social implications regarding her decision to have unprotected premarital sex for the first time and anytime thereafter. Just dealing solely with the door that we single women open unto contracting sexually transmitted diseases, this should be enough to make us want to delve into and expose why we put our lives at risk at all for pleasures' sake in the first place. The behavior is all the more daunting when multiple partners are added into the equation, as the chances now become higher for the woman to contract a disease and/or become pregnant. It is once with child and the decisions that then ensue that actually prompted the premise of this study. **WHEN** the woman decides to bring the baby to term in a live birth *(1.2 million women per year terminate their pregnancies)* **AND** opts to raise the child outside of a committed live-in relationship with the biological father as noted by Professor Patrick, this is when another "baby mama" is born. And considering that most baby mamas are not financially solid at the time of the child's birth, this study will prove how all unwed mothers are in some way or another responsible for the perpetuation of our nation's long-term social problems associated with growing up in fatherless homes. Consequently, an in-depth look into this phenomena surrounding America's "baby mama" craze will not only reveal how the woman's choice in this matter affects her as an individual, but in some aspects, the very choice to become a baby mama also impinges upon our country as well in six key areas:

- Social
- Spiritual
- Financial
- Physical
- Emotional
- Personal

By exploring a list ranging from social to personal concerns and doing so without the aide of rose-colored glasses, we will be able to pinpoint remedies to what sexually ails mankind.

In the perfect world, where a woman is not subject to the sexual assault of rapists, pedophiles, molesters, pimps, sex traffickers, or any other kind of deviant, women (unbeknownst to many of them) actually control sex. Yet with such power comes great responsibility, so the burning question is what do we women do with them both?

Here's a radical thought...... (*I am sure some may feel this idea is either antiquated or unrealistic*).... How about we women start taking responsibility by obeying the laws of God as concerned with sex? Do you know that **IF** all sexual abuse was eradicated and **IF** all women in this country would take a vow to keep their sexuality under wraps until marriage as well as exercise fidelity thereafter, social issues that plague our nation would completely vanish in time:

- Babies born out-of-wedlock as well as the bondage to the sin that drives inappropriate sexual unions would become a thing of the past.

- Sexually transmitted diseases would drastically decline and eventually die with the host .

- Female prostitution would be eliminated immediately.

- The internet could only circulate vintage woman-based pornography.

- The welfare system would no longer be drained to take care of "outside" children.

- Every child would know their lineage so paternity shows would disappear.

- Every heterosexual male would be held accountable, knowing that if he wanted to have sex with a woman, he would have to marry one.

- Marriages would no longer be the exception to our *new* rule, and our nation would benefit both from the return to the strength of solid, Godly families and from the eradication of sexual disease as well.

Sounds like something that could never happen?... Human beings actually living in peace without sexual sin?.... Sounds just like heaven on earth to me!

> **Babymamamania-** A sweeping craze whereby women who have babies out-of-wedlock, psychologically impose upon the biological father to care for a child he had no intention of fathering and/or does not want to financially support.

Ladies, please come to grips with this fact: if you are prepared to become a baby mama, you must also be prepared to raise that child without any help from the baby daddy. When our courts are overwhelmed with the chore of having to intervene in custody battles and enforce child support payments, do not **expect** *that your situation will be any different. Please understand that just because a man got you pregnant, this does not necessarily mean he will want to give you any money or be in the life of your child. The harsh reality is that you cannot force the baby daddy to care about a child especially when he may not even remember having sex with you or may want to forget that he had.*

As has been exposed on the Maury Show along with our own witness, many biological fathers do not willingly or consistently give up the needed cash as we assume he would want to. Whether he had sex with the baby mama only once or a lot, we cannot expect that he will want to be emotionally tied to a child that he is only legally financially responsible for. In all honesty, does it really serve the well being of the child when forced into the life of a man who could care less? The baby mama should just resolve that if he doesn't desire to know his own flesh and blood, it's her baby daddy's problem. If he chooses not to love the child beyond mandated child support, let it be. Pursuing a relationship beyond what the biological father is willing to allow is risky for all concerned, especially when the baby mama is doing so in order to stay connected to the daddy. Even more troubling is the fact her sole reason for pressing the matter is the only way to justify her choice of giving the *cookie* (as described by comedian Steve Harvey) to a man that was not her husband or worse yet, to one she did not really know. Whatever the motivation, the truth remains the truth… we cannot force someone to do something they do not want to do; God doesn't even force us, and He can.

You can bring a horse to the water,

but you can't make it drink.

-Anonymous

Social

Within the ignorance of my youth, I remember watching the *I Love Lucy* show, trying to figure how *White* parents- who slept in separate twin beds- could make babies when they did not sleep together as did my parents? As I got older and television censorship became more lax by the time Carol and Mike Brady shared the same bed, I would later recognize the power of the media's influence upon my psyche. I actually believed what I was shown concerning White America sexuality. Evidently, the extent of my knowledge about sex as young teen was regulated both by what my parents did or did not talk about and what I saw on TV. During my formative years, the media did not convey overtly sexual information and if celebrities were impregnated outside the bonds of marriage,

23

the media-of-old did not promote the "scandals" in the current manner that has evolved primarily due to the advances in technology. What was once a deep dark secret now gets you and the bastard child on the front cover of magazines worldwide! And I might add that sex was not as blatant in our music either. Young people today might find it hard to believe one could actually enjoy music that had no curse word or explicitly sexual lyrics. What has our society evolved to when one can hear the antics over the airwaves "*your neighbors know my name*" or "*you gonna think I invented sex….*"?

It was during my children's generation that I began to find it necessary to block certain cable stations to my home and monitor the radio in the car because of the *marginal* sexual innuendos. However, now that I am a grandparent, it is virtually impossible to live in this county outside of your own cocoon-of-a-home and not be buffeted about the head with SEX, SEX, SEX! Because of the intrusive nature of the media in general, blissful ignorance in our society is definitely a notion of the past. All things considered, are we then surprised that the United States' rate of unplanned pregnancies (*a pregnancy that is either mistimed or unwanted at the time of conception*) is higher than the world average, and much higher than that in any other industrialized nation? Is it a wonder that perhaps the sexual saturation found on the TV, the radio, the internet, on cell phones and in the newsprint contributes to the fact that almost half a million U.S. teens give birth each year as reported by the American Pregnancy Association? Most startling probably is the fact that White America is now experiencing the same social troubles associated with this behavior once thought to be only indicative by race or social stature.

While socially, the baby mama will always be branded as such if she never marries the father of her child, it is her *decision* to actually become a baby mama that is much more detrimental upon the environment in which she lives. In view of the fact that the building block of a society is the nucleus family, it is important to see how the progressive change in our country's views on sex is altering this very footprint for future generations. By enveloping the choice of the baby mama to create fatherless homes, our country is now moving away from our blueprint of the traditional family- a blueprint that has been intact for most Americans since the pilgrims landed on Plymouth Rock. And as the broken home is now trending to become the norm, this very change presents foundation-rocking implications for American life. We must be prepared to absorb on a grander scale the negative consequences that arise from children being raised without their biological fathers in the home, and even more devastating, without the fathers in their lives at all.

Although the traditional mold for the American family may not be the assumed choice any longer- particularly when legislation recently passed changing the guidelines for who can now marry- the broken home is nothing new for Black America. Black families in general historically have never been what our nation considers whole or fixed. Despite the concerted efforts of many Black people for a semblance of family life in their hopes of achieving their American Dream too, there are definite lengths of time encompassing particular events in our history that have influenced the actual yet unfortunate fragility of the Black family:

The Institution

Slavery, in itself, did not allow for the formation of stable Black families in this country from the onset of our arrival primarily due to their inability to legally marry. When masters would permit slaves to "jump the broom", generally it was understood that the male slave could only continue to cohabitate with his woman if he consistently produced seed. Also, it was not uncommon for him to be assigned a different woman for every night of the week or "exchanged" when he failed to impregnate any of them. In addition, there was always the possibility that on any given night the overseer may want the slave's woman for himself or perhaps the master would need to sell either of them to settle a debt. As the proverbial straw to the camel's back, since slave children (the institution's highest commodity) were generally sold or traded

27

once weaned, Black families found it difficult to solidify while living under the constant threat of separation and invasion.

The Emancipation

The years immediately following 1863 were some of the most dangerous for Black families in our country. No longer covered under slave laws as items of property, scores of Black men were pulled from their tenant farmhouses, strung up in neighboring trees, tortured, emasculated and usually burned before a crowd of cheering White Americans. Without any legal recourse for criminal prosecution or protection in part due to the introduction of the Jim Crow laws, women and children were left behind to fend for themselves, thus creating a vast number of what we now refer to as single-parent households. As cries for justice rang strong because of *new* horrors faced by the former slaves- cries that fell upon deaf ears- countless Black families wished to be returned to the solace and pseudo-security of captivity.

The Migration

It would be the lure of financial freedom and escape from the widespread violence of lynchings as well as the Jim Crow laws that would incite over 1.4 million Blacks to move into large industrialized northern cities between the years of 1910 to 1930. This movement from the former slave-holding states on the surface presented new-found opportunities for Black men to find work with the railroads, stockyards and meatpacking plants recruiting heavily from the south with discounted tickets and false incentives. Because no expectations were realized for the government's assistance with the migration of a people not so long ago oppressed, separation within the feeble Black family continued as most men were forced to leave their families behind until they were stable enough to send for them. However, when Black migrants were met by the ever-prevailing racism thought to have been contained only within the south, the transition from rural farmer to urban industrial worker proved to be too daunting of a task for many, and the assurances of reconciliation for the family "up north" began to wane.

The System

By the late 1950s and 1960s, Blacks were more densely concentrated in inner cities than any other group due primarily to housing discrimination practices following the great migration north of just one generation earlier. Unfortunately for any location that houses concentrated bodies, poverty and crime are soon close at hand. To combat the rising social concerns generating from what we now call the "projects", President Lyndon B. Johnson enacted a set of domestic programs called the *Great Society.* This legislation was proposed solely for the elimination of poverty and racial injustice through social reforms. Because of these programs, for the first time in our country, a person who was not elderly or disabled could receive a living from the American government. This included general welfare payments, health care through Medicaid, food stamps, special payments for pregnant women and young mothers as well as federal and state housing benefits. While the reforms were crucial and beneficial for most of the individuals on what Americans refer to as "welfare", the already fragile Black family continued to be manipulated by the new system that conversely presented a further threat to family solidarity by providing financial stability. The issue was this- in order for a woman to receive free money from the government to help her care for underage children, there could be no employable male over the age of 18 in the household. A choice was now forced upon the family: would the woman run the risk of prosecution for fraud and repayment of all monies granted to her by having the father of her children live illegally in the home with them? Or would the two parents honor God, get married, earn honest wages instead of defrauding the government, financially support their own children themselves, and by being an example of stability for their kids, finally break the generational curse of the broken Black home?....

That's too much like right!

Spiritual

The illusion of sexual freedom is just that, an illusion. This false and misleading impression of reality is actually twofold regarding our country's wide-spread acceptance of "freedom" for all sexual unions. American people in general have now come to believe that it okay to have babies out-of-wedlock AND that homosexuality must be okay too since many states– including the Nation's Capitol – have ratified legislation allowing for same sex marriages. **For the record, neither has been, is, nor ever will be okay with God.** Whether an individual likes having sex with people that have the same or different body parts - if there is no Holy union between the two - it is sin. And no matter how many laws are passed in this land "licensing" sinful relations, God's law will not transform. The fact that our country's formative documents such as the Declaration of Independence, the Constitution and Bill of Rights were carefully scripted under the influence of the Holy Bible, I would imagine our founding fathers must be turning over in their graves to know that the country they forged under God's teachings has all but abandoned the source for the sake of pleasure alone.

From the beginning, God created sexual relations and procreation specifically for marriage. As His rules have not changed, human behavior has. In biblical times, there were only four categories of non-slave women as related to sexuality: the **virgin**, the **wife**, the **widow** and the **harlot** (the latter whose group included the adulteress, lesbian and prostitute) Godly rules and regulations closely governed respectively the sexual behaviors of these groups of women, and most of the biblical mandates brought with them the death penalty for violating what we now accept as common practice. The biblical sexuality breakdown is as follows:

The virgin had no sex
The wife had only marital sex,
The widow usually had no more sex
The harlot had sex with everybody else!

Today however, the freedom of sexual activities for unmarried women has created a newly formed category – the *"Single Lady"*- (*She's emancipated, makes her own money; has her own place; and she identifies proudly with this sassy title made popular by Beyonce*). In reality, her practice of premarital sex places her into only one of the four biblical groups listed, yet one will find that most single ladies won't accept God's title primarily because they don't sleep around **that** much….

Given how God still views sexuality, the burning question remains why do so many women today make the decision to have unprotected premarital sex despite all the risks involved? Even more poignantly, why do single *Christian* women choose to fornicate when possessing at least an adequate knowledge of what is sin and the associated consequences? The answer to this question is both complex and yet very simple: Plainly speaking, consensual sex feels good… if it didn't, we would not be in the mess we are in right now. Yet the complications surrounding the decision to have sex outside of the bonds of marriage arises as lines between nature's urges and the truth become blurred. As single Christian women, we are expected to know that engaging in any type of sexual practices outside of the bonds of marriage is wrong and are supposed to follow the teachings of Jesus on the subject matter by acting accordingly. Romans 8:3 tells us:

For what the law could not do, in that it was weak through the flesh, God sending his own Son in the likeness of sinful flesh, and for sin, condemned sin in the flesh.

With the added knowledge that God's anointing and blessing is not upon any un-godly sexual union, the question that remains is why do *we* do it? As multifaceted are the motives why any single lady has sex (low self-esteem, loneliness, neediness, perversions and seductions etc), for the Christian woman, all of these reasons simply boil down to one final decision in whether or not to "go all the way" – it is because the desire at that particular moment is to please the flesh more that to please

God. As 1 Corinthians 14:40 reveals *"Let **all** things be done decently and in order"*, We Christians know that premarital sex is neither decent nor in order. We are also aware of the biblical example in which God brought vengeance against two cites for among other things, sexual immorality:

> **2 Peter 2:6 And [God] turning the cities of Sodom and Gomorrah into ashes condemned them with an overthrow, making them an ensample unto those that after should live ungodly.**

> **Jude 1:7 Even as Sodom and Gomorrah, and the cities about them in like manner, giving themselves over to fornication, and going after strange flesh, are set forth for an example, suffering the vengeance of eternal fire.**

If our God would completely destroy cities as an example to the ungodly, just think of what His judgment will be against an entire *nation* that continues to exploit, participate in, accept, and refuse to control sexual sin? Even though it may be hard to live celibate, it is not impossible. If we

36

Christian women won't get it together, we will continue to fail each other and fail as a strong example to the non-believer. How effectively can we express to a nation literally dying from within of the importance of "One Nation Under God " when **we** don't even conquer our own sin? Good news though, God provided a path to healing when He delivered a nation of people out from captivity, leading them through the wilderness and into the Promised Land as a sign of salvation to the world. For when we as a nation of women truly heal, particularly the nation of Black women, mending and restoration will not only come to our families, but to our communities and our country as well.

> *...If My people who are called by My name will humble themselves, and pray and seek My face, and turn from their wicked ways, then I will hear from heaven, and will forgive their sin and heal their land.*
> **2 Chronicles 7:14**

With all being said, first I want to challenge the nation of Christian women to consider making a **V.OW.** from this point forward to keep sex only within the bonds of marriage as the Bible instructs. Once we make the choice to live in **Victory** **Over** **Wickedness** (**V.O.W.**), we will stop being a horrible witness to the saving power of Jesus whenever we find ourselves panting underneath men who are not our husbands. And if those men are also our brothers in Christ, I challenge them to consider their witness as well and make the decision to honor our God, our **V.O.W.** *and* our bodies by getting married as our Father expects.

Secondly, I challenge the nation of Black women to make the **V.O.W.** and give the Black family the prospect of finally living free from under the curses of brokenness and malady.

Lastly, I challenge the nation of American women to make the **V.O.W.** thus helping our country realize a substantial decrease in babies born out-of-wedlock and sexually transmitted diseases by the 2020 Census.

> *Ultimately if we all get it together my sisters, God promised He would heal our land. And with that healing, our nation can then help heal the world.*

And the dream we're conceived in
will reveal a joyful face;
And the world we once believed in
will shine again in grace....
Heal the world; make it a better place
for you and for me and the entire human race.

"Heal the World" – Michael Jackson

Financial

When I became a pregnant teenager almost thirty years ago, I was required to "put" my baby daddy on child support as stipulated by the welfare department. He was ordered to pay $50 per month because I was on public assistance, so the government garnished his minuscule paycheck on my behalf. About half-way through college, I made the decision to get off aid when his frequent visits would become a permanent living situation- my child's father and I started to make marriage plans for when I graduated. Even though the frequent cheating and beatings would follow me onto grad school, I was still yet purposed in my heart to marry him because I didn't want to be considered a "statistic". I felt that if I *did* marry my daughter's father, it would prove to my parents and my community I really wasn't like those *other* girls that got pregnant in high school. However, it wasn't until he stabbed at me with a pair of scissors that I realized a life with him was definitely out of the question. As I soon found it necessary to withdraw from the master's program at San Diego State University in an attempt to gain order in my life, can you imagine my surprise as I tried to obtain child support from my child's father, I learned that he would not be required to pay more than the $50 per month that had been initiated by the welfare department because I made more money than he. And coupled with the fact that social services informed me they would not spend the man hours to enforce such a nominal amount... that I would have to do all the leg work myself to collect the money... I never pursued the matter, resolving myself to support her on my own. I figured that if my baby daddy wouldn't willingly pay the $50 in support, he definitely would not be worth any energy to enforce the collection. However for the sake of our daughter, I knew I could not react like some who feel when the father doesn't pay support, he shouldn't be able see his child. What good would it have done for my daughter to keep her from her father because he was not a good provider? And given his untimely death in 2007, I am blessed when I look back on my decision: even though my baby daddy rarely gave me any money, he saw our daughter almost every single week during her childhood and teen years. Because I had encouraged a relationship between them as she grew up, my daughter could be comforted in his passing knowing that he indeed loved her.

As was in my case, for women who never are not married to the fathers of their children, matters of finances generally defaults to the public welfare system- a system that requires paternity be established in order to make certain the father's *legal* role in financially supporting their child and in reimbursing the government for taking care of their seed. And as the welfare system's health care costs rise due to the increasing amount of women having children outside of marriage, it is evident by the sheer numbers there is no real forethought for most women into the absolute prevention of pregnancy or its probable affect on the economic stability for herself, her child or her society. As many baby mamas find themselves struggling to raise their children with little or no physical help from the biological father, had there never been a committed relationship between the two, she may find it impossible to collect money from him at all; this task could even be considered futile if the baby daddy has a brood already. (*I am always amazed by the Maury show when the baby mama admits she knew her man he had double-digit kids prior to them making yet another*). The fact that many men do not pay child support or do not pay it willingly has become a rapidly growing, cancerous condition for our country as it reveals a ghastly undermining of strength for the family and the wholeness of children. I am sure we all know at least one man shirking his financial responsibilities to children he fathered. Moreover, if it happened to be your own father, you could probably fill the pages of this book with story-after-story of the problems encountered as a child due to his lack of help or support. To illuminate this mounting concern for our country, following are the nationwide Child Support Statistics and Trends as tabulated from our last census. By 2002:

- Only 62.6% of court-ordered Child Support payments were received

- 31.2% of custodial mothers have never been married

- 84% of child support providers were men

- South Dakota lead our nation with a collection rate of 83% of child support payments due (the national average is 53%)

- Hawaii and the District of Columbia tied for the lowest collection rate in our country at * **22**%.

I am so glad to know of a Black man who in spite of only remembering seeing his own father but once when he was 10 years old, has broken the generational curse for his own family and stands before us as a phenomenal example of both husband and father… even though this man was born in one of the places with the lowest collection rate and runs the nation from the other- (Barack Obama-44th U.S. President)

At the time of this writing, our nation is within a few years from the tabulated results that will follow the 2010 census. Now, I cannot guarantee that the problems have gotten any worse over the past 10 years, but I am assured they didn't get any better as has been exposed on shows like that of Maury's. For those of my readers that are astonished like me by the findings listed, set yourself up a reminder and be sure to visit the Census Bureau's website to note if there were any major fluctuations in the nation's relative numbers as discussed- definitely considering the spurt in babies as a result of our nation's baby mama craze. Unfortunately, as has been revealed by the disheartening stats, a fact will yet remain within the next findings- many father's deposit into the lives of their children was merely into the child's mother at the time of conception.

> **Babymamamania-** The belief in the absurd notion if a man has unprotected sex with a woman, he must want her to be his baby mama, otherwise he would have used protection .

Ladies, even though we know that pillow talk will sometimes include utterances referencing "making a baby", don't assume that the man you are having unprotected sex with will want to be there for your child even if he promised during the heat of passion. Evidently the need to have his biological urge satisfied is much greater than making sure no children will come from the union- children he would and should be expected to financially and emotionally support. Since the thought process for both of you is all about the moment and not necessarily the outcome nine months later, you must understand that some men will say whatever you want to hear in order to get everything you are willing to give them.

Physical

Though it seems to sooth our social conscious if the Maury Show can at least help some baby mamas find an answer regarding the paternity for their child, what we really need to address are the particular consequences than result from the reason *why* they do not know. Because these baby mamas chose to have unprotected sex with multiple partners, they have also placed at risk the well-being and possibly the lives of her partners and her children as well. Somehow, we as a nation must tackle such a stronghold whereby single women would even allow different men to have sex with her without at least using condoms. And while the Center for Disease Control and Prevention (CDC) reports that more than half of U.S. women have had an unplanned pregnancy by the age of 45, some groups such as teens (the part of our society that is generally bombarded sun-up-to-sun-down with sexual infiltration) are at a higher increased risk of morbidity and pregnancy health behaviors that can adversely effect the health of the infant as well.

Staggering is the fact that with about 3 million teens acquiring a sexually transmitted disease (STD) each year, yet more frightening is their destructive sexual behavior's dire impositions upon the general population. Here are the disturbing tabulations from the CDC's 2008 Sexually Transmitted Disease Surveillance Study regarding the general population within the continental United States of American and her territories:

- In 2008 there were more than 68 million individuals living with a STD- sexually transmitted disease.

- The largest number of reported cases of both Chlamydia and Gonorrhea in 2008 was among girls between 15 and 19 years of age, followed closely by young women 20 to 24 years of age.

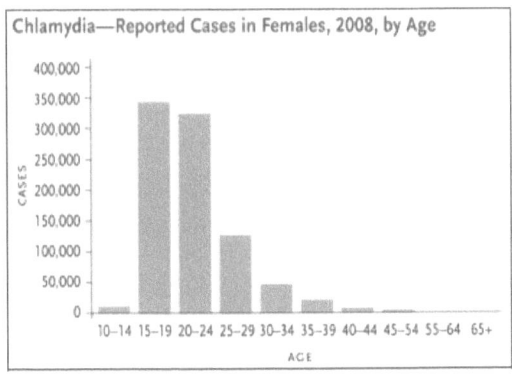

Chlamydia—Reported Cases in Females, 2008, by Age

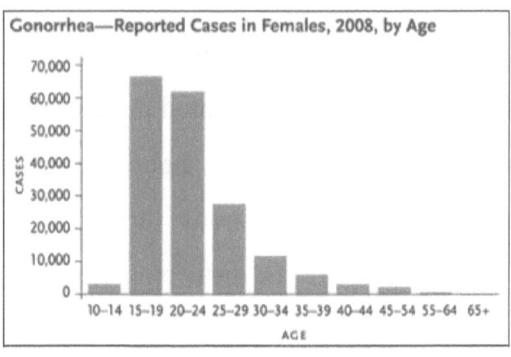

Gonorrhea—Reported Cases in Females, 2008, by Age

- Black people represent only 12 percent of the total U.S. population, but made up more than 70 percent of gonorrhea cases.

- The Chlamydia rate among Blacks in 2008 was more than eight times higher than that of Whites.

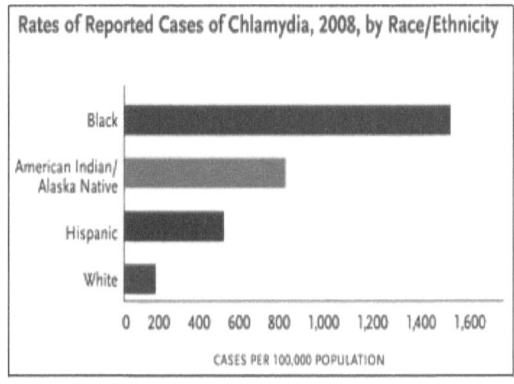

Rates of Reported Cases of Chlamydia, 2008, by Race/Ethnicity

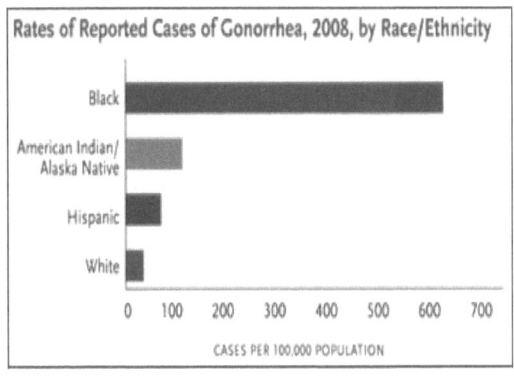

Rates of Reported Cases of Gonorrhea, 2008, by Race/Ethnicity

CASES PER 100,000 POPULATION

**It must be noted that socioeconomic barriers to quality healthcare and STD prevention and treatment services are a likely contributor to higher STD rates among racial and ethnic minorities.

Although technically considered an STD, HIV/AIDS can also be contracted from other sources, such as sharing injection drug syringes with someone who has HIV. Yet, having unprotected sex is still the primary behavioral risk factor for becoming infected, and of all racial and ethnic groups in the United States, HIV and AIDS have hit Black America the hardest. According to the CDC, in 2007:

- Blacks accounted for 51% of the estimated 35,962 new AIDS cases diagnosed in the 50 states and the District of Columbia

- For both Black men and women, the most common way of contracting HIV was having unprotected sex with another man who had HIV.

- 63% of children under the age of 13 diagnosed with HIV/AIDS were Black.

- Blacks accounted for 44% of the 455,636 people living with AIDS in the 50 states and District of Columbia

- The rate of AIDS diagnoses for Black men was almost 8 times the rate for White men

- The rate of AIDS diagnoses for Black women was 22 times the rate for White women.

- By the end of 2007, 40% of the 562,793 persons with AIDS who died were Black

Below is the chart based on Race/ethnicity of persons diagnosed with HIV/AIDS during 2007:

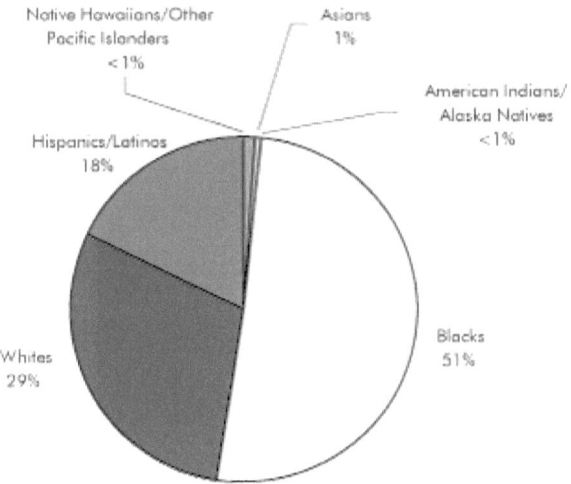

Here are the CDC's charts illustrating American's **living** with HIV/AIDS as compared by gender:

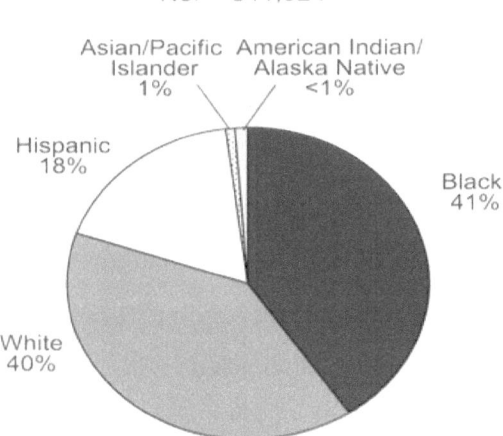

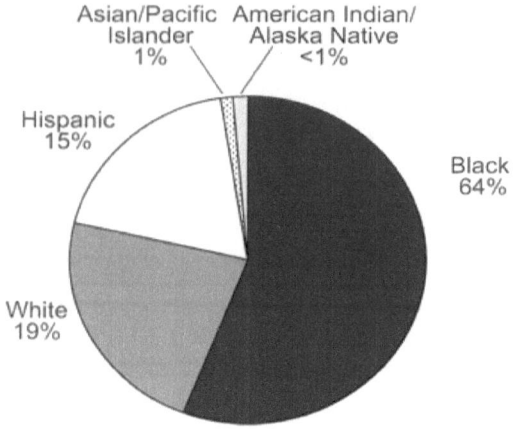

Females
No. = 126,964

Asian/Pacific Islander 1%

American Indian/ Alaska Native <1%

Hispanic 15%

Black 64%

White 19%

**HIV/AIDS remains a leading cause of death for Black America, particularly for those at highest risk- the 25% of the Black population that live in poverty.

Using the evidence presented from the Center for Disease Control and Prevention, it can actually be established who represents the most dangerous person to have unprotected sex within the continental United States of America and her surrounding territories. It should also be illuminated that the following findings are tabulated from those that actually *went* to clinics to be treated for the various symptoms associated with some STDs. How daunting this fact is for our nation considering the scores of women that do not know they carry a disease nor care that they do. Who represents that dangerous group? She is the **young Black female between the ages of 15 and 24....**

> *...And the diagrams on the following pages will reveal to you where she resides!*

Gonorrhea - Positivity among 15-to 24-year-old women tested in family planning clinics by state.

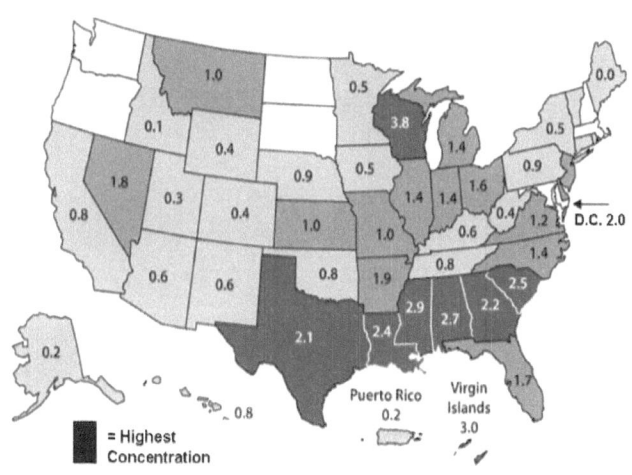

- Wisconsin ranked the highest 3.8% of its population of women 15-24 years of age infected with Gonorrhea.

- Texas, Louisiana, Mississippi, Alabama, Georgia and South Carolina have the most concentrated cases of Gonorrhea.

Chlamydia—Positivity among 15- to 24-year-old women tested in family planning clinics by state .

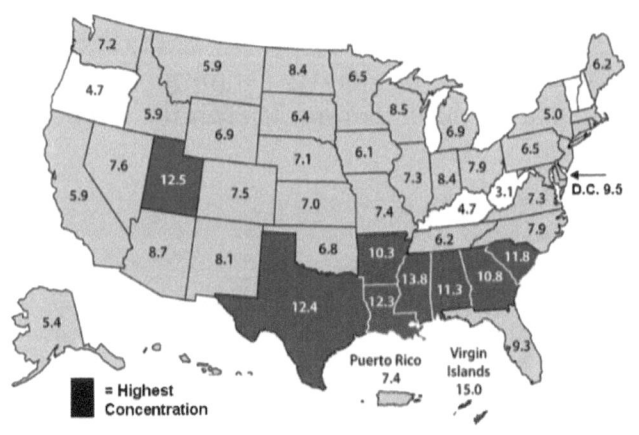

- The Virgin Islands ranked the highest with 15% of its population of women 15-24 years of age infected . with Chlamydia.

- Mississippi ranked highest within the continental United States with 13.8%

- Texas, Louisiana, Mississippi, Alabama, Georgia and South Carolina have the most concentrated cases of Chlamydia

- The highest threat of all 15-24 year old women, whereby **both** Chlamydia and Gonorrhea can be contracted lives in the Virgin Islands.

It is my hope that you are just as mortified as I am to learn the devastating news concerning the sexuality of our nation. Even more importantly, I pray that these appalling statistics I have shared will motivate both an individual and a collective sexual behavior modification: It may be quite possible that Christian readers are now convicted in the sin and will do the right thing and **stop** having premarital sex... Maybe young women will see that by practicing celibacy, they can altogether eliminate their risk of being a host of the sex-related ailments that plague our society.... Conceivably men who cannot contain themselves until marriage and continue to *"hook up"* with women who are not willing to change their destructive behavior, should begin to now check for both jail-bait age **and** hometown... Should any adjustments come to pass, there will be one much-need result that will be common for all- a drastic reduction in babies born out-of-wedlock. With all that said, I do know one thing for sure; considering the concentration of STDs from Texas to South Carolina, we won't think of the phrase "**the Dirty South**" the same way ... ever again!

Babymamamania- The widespread fallacy that if a man continues to have sex on a regular basis with his baby mama, he must still have feelings for her.

This goes out to all my baby mamas....
...It's about time we had our own song
Don't know what took so long
'Cause now-a-days it's like a badge of honor
to be a baby mama.

'Baby Mama'- Fantasia Barrino

A neighbor once invited me over for some holiday cheer and upon arrival to his apartment, I could not help but notice the pornographic movie in full assault smeared all over his big screen TV. Following my expression to him regarding this uncomfortable situation, he reluctantly changed it to a football game. I then questioned him as to why he didn't feel the movie would not have offended me. He responded with the typical "because we are grown" and continued to inform me that generally when women are invited to his bachelor pad, "they know what's up" and if the women can't accept this, then they can't come over. I shared with my neighbor that any woman who would agree to this type of situation is not whole. He then shocked me with his honesty in telling me that he doesn't want a whole woman, because a whole woman wants the commitment he is not willing to ever give. As I happily excused myself, the dead bolt clicking behind me, I realized, it's a WHOLE woman that he really seeks....

If a man like this sounds familiar to you- if you are summonsed on your particular night to come and do your particular thing for him- don't get it twisted; you may have been just the most convenient, live receptacle that evening.

Emotional

I adopted the attitude early on as a parent that my kids were *my* kids and if anyone didn't want to do anything for them that was fine with me.

Even more important, if a person wouldn't provide for *all* of my kids (clothes, toys, money etc), I made it very clear I expected that individual not to do anything for any of them. This applied to everyone, but in particular to my baby daddy and my ex-husband. Since my children have different fathers, I wanted to prevent the added psychological damage caused by one father doing for his child(ren) only and the kids having to compare between the two. Fortunate for me, neither father really outshined the other, so this was relatively easy to accomplish. Also, in my children's favor was that they never had to bear the shame of being denied by their fathers or from not knowing who he was since paternity was never in question. As this was the only arena in which I had control over- regulating who could give to my children- it was imperative that I spared them any additional pain; they had enough to deal with. My children were already wrestling with emotional issues surrounding their respective relationship with their fathers and the problems ran the gamut for my four: abandonment, rejection, disappointment, neglect, distress, instability, disillusionment... the list goes on. So by adding fuel to the fire disguised in the comparisons between the two fathers would have been more than any of us could bear. Unfortunately, like many other children in this county, they too we subjected to countless broken promises and shattered expectations. As such, I never felt the need to say anything to my children concerning their negligent, dead-beat fathers; they saw that for themselves. Most of my time was actually spent trying to mend their brokenness

In spite of all that most children go through because of their deficient fathers, nothing however seems to cause more emotional damage to their well-being than living with a dejected mother. When a baby mama is angry because of child support and/or rejection issues and does not contain her rage nor conceal her bitterness from the child, Pandora's Box will open. (*We have seen such rage time and time again on the Maury show as insults and furniture fly across his stage*). And when that box finally opens, one of two things generally occurs: the child will either learn to resent their father or come to resent their mother for her relentlessly berating of him. Whichever is the outcome; all of this could have been avoided if the baby mama would have been mature enough to keep her emotions in check for the sake of the child's sanity. Instead of expending every needed effort to soothe her child's prevailing heart and soul aches, angered baby mamas actually compound already fragile family matters. No good can ever come from the baby mama's tirade of verbal, emotional and/or physically abuse directed at the baby daddy IN FRONT OF THE CHILD- no matter how much money he owes her....no matter if he only uses her for sex. And whether her growing resentment continues to fester from regret for having sex with the baby daddy either initially or continuously, the baby mama must be careful not to misplace and transfer the rage she feels towards him onto their child(ren) for some people never recover from childhood psychological and/or physical abuse from a parent. Behavior such as this makes it very apparent that years of living under the unbridled fury of a spurned mother can unleash unto society fractured young adults, and the emotional baggage these kids will drag behind them can only perpetuate the destructive generational curses in our country.

The baby mama's emotional baggage begins to surface when it becomes difficult for her to distinguish the thin line between love and lust. If the baby mama is dealing with issues of loneliness, continuing to have sex with her baby daddy might be the only way to have access to a handy, warm body. The problems arise when she begins to confuse convenience with anything beyond that. For those still looking for Prince Charming to come back for good and sweep her off her feet (like we saw on TV), she has a tendency to read too much into the baby daddy's visits, especially if he is involved with someone else. Or perhaps, the baby mama's self-esteem is so low, she believes the one-sided relationship with the baby daddy is the best she can do for herself. Maybe she is so needy that she is actually encourages the encounters as a means to end of the separation between the two, especially when she moves into seductive-mode to entice him to change his mind. And of course there's the chance that she is the lustful one and could care less if he had feelings for her or not, as long as she is "gettin' hers. Nonetheless, when the baby mama harbors any of the countless emotions stimulating her to give sexual favors to a man that refuses to commit, her baggage becomes evident when she refuses to accept that their union signifies anything meaningful beyond the very act itself. This becomes very clear particularly if more babies have been produced by the pair and a committed relationship is still not forged in spite of booty call, after booty call, after booty call.

Babymamamania- The pop-culture trend of single mothers referring to the baby daddy as a fiancé when there is neither engagement ring nor commitment in sight.

*To all my sistas.... stop trying to fix it up! 40 might be the new 20, but a "friend with benefits" who has not given you an engagement ring is **not** the new fiancé!*

Personal

With all that has been discussed within this social study of "Babymamamania" in the United States of America, the key areas of concern have illuminated:

- The social implications of the steady (if not increasing) amount of children born out of wedlock
- The spiritual consequenses of a nation wrapped in sexual sin
- The financial dilemma surrounding support for the outside child
- the physical ramifications of having unprotected sex
- the emotional reasons why single women have sex in the first place

Basically the baby mama needs take it "personal" if her child's father does not want to marry her and for the sake of principal alone, she should cut off the sex until he does. By continuing to allow the baby daddy to have sex with her... by holding onto a dream that a ring has not fulfilled.... the baby mama takes the lead in this *"bass akward"* relationship that allows men to have liberties with parts of her body they are not entitled to. It is my desire that the information presented in this study may have motivated some to take personal ownership of their contribution to what sexually ails society. From here, if we can take a good long honest look at ourselves in the mirror and with the help of God, make the necessary corrections to our behavior, we will then be on the right path to true healing as recovery can only begin with admission.

I'm starting with the man in the mirror
I'm asking him to change his ways
and no message could'a been any clearer-
If you wanna make the world a better place
take a look at yourself,
and then make a change.

"Man In The Mirror" – Michael Jackson

The Women of Proverbs 7

Anne

Antoinette

Ashley

Tonya

Ginni

Anne – needy

Even though she charged men to have sex, Anne didn't consider herself a prostitute. Just like before she got married, when she was short on her gas bill or maybe needed some groceries, she knew who to call. All she had to do was pretend she liked it…just like she used to pretend with her uncles and cousins and since they took it from her when she was a kid, she figured might as well get paid for it now. Unlike before, this time she was behind on her rent and most of her "*friends*" didn't have it like that- but there was always Daryl. It didn't matter to her that Daryl was bringing her to the Maury Show tomorrow, knowing all she would have to do is call.

Still frozen in thought on the edge of bed, Anne remembered the promise she made yesterday. She told her social worker that she would not trade sex for money again; she had even promised God. Then, Anne remembered her mother….

Lifting her eyes toward the tattered crib in

66

the corner, a wave of disappointment engulfed Anne because she had been doing so well…she was really trying to change. Slowly rising to go to her sleeping son, Anne tried to convince herself it would be okay... just this one last time. A single tear wiped the side of the little boy's forehead as she leaned in to tuck her brand-new robe around his plump frame. "Mommy won't be needing this on her trip after all" she whispered, as she kissed him gently and then just stared at him… she couldn't believe she could love someone so much.

Crossing over to the closet, Anne reached for the big green trash bag headed for the garbage and untied the knot. After rifling through its contents, she found the yellow thong…. Daryl liked yellow… so did her mother. "I needed you mama!" Anne shouted aloud, startling the sleeping child. Catching herself, she made her way quickly back to the crib to shake it gently and soothe the baby's whimpers. Wiping away the remnant of her tears and vowing to be a better mother than her own, Anne rested her hand on his tiny beating heart and assured her son, "I got you, son.. Momma got you!"

She is loud and defiant; her feet nevr stay at home;

Antoinette - nasty

As she pulled the covers over her body, Antoinette knew tomorrow her husband might leave her for good if the twins were not his. She tucked the blanket under the cushions of the hotel's couch, and thought about what her grandmother had said to her on the phone. *"Baby, now you know you don't look too bright goin' on Maury for the sixth time! You gonna lose that good man for sure this time, 'specially when you tell him the rest."* Antoinette agreed that Matthew indeed was a good man; not too many men would marry a woman with four baby daddies.

Just two days earlier, Antoinette had brought Matthew to the show to reveal the secret about the paternity of the twins; her guilt would not let her keep it in any longer. And because he had not spoken to her since the nurse swabbed his cheek, she thought it best to give him his space. Wrapped comfortably on the plush couch, Antoinette closed her eyes, hoping and praying the twins weren't Freddie's babies this time though. He had appeared on the first four Maury shows to be tested for her four other kids... she just couldn't leave Freddie alone- it is what it is. He knew how to scratch her itch and he was the best lover she ever had…. better than Matthew and definitely better than Sean.

A smile warmed Antoinette's face as she thought of Sean and their night together, remembering how nervous he was in the beginning. She just couldn't help herself, he was so cute and so inexperienced- the two things she really liked. Antoinette's countenance began to pale as her thoughts drifted to how she probably blew it with Matthew for sure. Because she had sex with all three men around the time she got pregnant, once again, she didn't know who the father was. *"Oh well!"* she rehearsed in her mind as she floated off to sleep. *"That's right, I got it like that!"* She knew the crowd would boo her again, but she didn't care. *"Whateva!"*… Yep, Antoinette was ready to face them again; she just wished she hadn't hurt Matthew along the way- he really was a good man.

She took hold of him and kissed him and with a brazen face
she said: I have fellowship offerings at home;
Today I fulfilled my vows .So I came out to meet you;
I looked for you and have found you!

Proverbs 7:13- 15

Ashley - low self esteem

When his mother was not around, Malik was Ashley's knight in shining armor. From the first day they met, he had been supportive and caring and she was in love with him for that. As Ashley kneeled along side her dilapidated futon, she remembered the first time Malik prayed with her when she was living in the women's shelter. Even though she thought he was so cute as he taught the Sunday School lesson part of his mama's prison ministry, it was his answer to Ashley's question that would change the course of her life forever - " *If I done a lot of bad things with men...why would Jesus want to forgive me"*

While situating her knees comfortably on the old shag carpet, Ashley thought about the bittersweet moment when Malik lead her to Christ on that afternoon, for she was sure Malik could never be interested in girl like her now that he knew her past. As she clasped her hands together in her nightly prayer and leaned forward onto the mattress, Ashley looked toward heaven with a smile on her lips, "Look at us now, Lord" she began her prayer.

"Tomorrow God, I gotta go to the Maury show 'cause of Malik's mama, and I need your help. I wish I would'na kept asking him for more sex 'cause now we got this baby to take care of. God, *please* don't let his mama say nothin' stupid to me! And please help her accept her grandson when she finally knows the truth so she could let us be a family for real.

"I thank you Lord for Malik. When I sometimes don't feel good 'bout myself cause of things I done…I can call Malik and when he come by to show me love, he always tellin' me that Jesus loves me *anyway* and *anyhow*. I know Malik loves me and the baby too, even though he ain't never said it. I thank you that he still wanna marry me when he finish school, 'cause he tell me every time he come around. He gonna be a good husband to me when his mama get out of the way….In Jesus' name pray, Amen…. Oh yea Lord, sorry for having sex."

71

I have covered my bed with colored linens from Egypt.
I have perfumed my bed with myrrh, aloes and cinnamon.
Come, let's drink deep of love till morning;
Let's enjoy ourselves with love!

Proverbs 7:16- 18

Tonya - lonely

Tonya was in love with Sean. Period. She couldn't help it because her heart still belonged to him and it didn't matter to Tonya that he was engaged to Mary. With shaking hands, she grabbed her duffle bag and keys, knowing within a matter of hours, she would have the truth about the baby.

Tonya didn't look forward to the four-hour drive to the Maury Show because she knew that she wouldn't be able to stop thinking about Sean the whole trip…. thinking about how he made her feel. Usually, when she and Patrick had their spats and she needed some "company", she'd make the call, light the scented candles, and wait anxiously for the cell phone signal that he was here. But the last time they had sex, she had to actually beg Sean to come to her for her birthday. This never happened before, so she figured that he really must have feelings for his new girlfriend. And since they shared a long history of lovemaking

72

and two kids, Tonya was surprised that he would even make her beg in the first place; she thought they were *like that*. She remembered how pathetic she sounded as she pleaded for his sex. However, it was following her many unreturned phone calls and text messages, that she finally got the picture- Sean had made it very clear that all he wanted to talk about from now on was just his kids.

As her heart began to pound in her throat, Tonya realized her excitement about seeing Sean again. She missed him terribly and wondered did he even miss her at all... did he at least miss their sex because she sure did. Ever since she told Sean that he might be the father of her youngest daughter also, he started having his mama come and pick the kids up for him. Tonya felt that given their past, he didn't have to do that with the kids and he definitely didn't have to cut her off like that. "*I bet that Mary got something to do with this, like she gonna keep him away from me when this baby turns out to be his too.*" Noticing she was still stuck in thought standing at the front door, Tonya nervously stepped through to possess her destiny.

"My husband is not at home; he has gone on a long journey.
He took his purse filled with money and
will not be home till full moon."
With persuasive words she led him astray;
she seduced him with her smooth talk

Proverbs 7:19-21

Ginni – seductress

The tinted window on the Cadillac limousine rolled down slowly revealing Ginni checking her make-up. Barely looking up from her chore, she shouted Tyrone's way, "And make sure that all your clothes are removed from the basement storage unit. I want to make sure you have no reason to come back to *my* house." As she returned her attention back to the make-up compact, Ginni instructed the driver to close the window and make haste to the airport. Oblivious to her stunned husband running alongside the luxurious vehicle, still trying to make sense of the bombshell that was dropped last night, Ginni's focus remained solely on the plan despite of all the pounding on the window and Tyrone's attempts to open the limo's door... Things were finally coming together for Ginni.

As she began to apply her mascara, she caught a glimpse of Tyrone in the small mirror, collapsing to his knees in the middle of the street with his head in his hands. She watched his reflection become smaller and smaller and then finally disappear as she pondered little about their discussion last night; he just didn't seem to take it too well.

Ginni had decided to pack his belongings while he was away on business, but when Tyrone returned home a few days earlier as surprise- roses and champagne in hand- Ginni simply handed him the note she had already prepared, detailing the affair with her ex-husband Pastor Johnson. As Tyrone's suspicions were confirmed by her heartless hand-written account of her infidelity, Ginni just continued to pack for her trip; making sure to relieve him of the bottle of bubbly so she could have something to celebrate with following her expected news at the Maury Show. Despite her husband's tearful pleas for an explanation, she felt there was no need for any further discussion on the matter since it was all in the letter. "*He's the one making it hard on himself*", Ginni muttered, snapping the compact shut. She was done.

BABYMAMAMANIA

*[bey-bee-mah-muh-**mey**-nee-uh]* - (**noun**)

Cast of Characters

STAGE MANAGER #1

STAGE MANAGER #2

HEAD STAGEHAND

TONYA

SEAN

DIANE

DANCERS

ASHLEY

BRIDGETT

MARGARITA

MALIK

DARYL

ANNE

C.K.SHA'

MATTHEW

ANTOINETTE

YANA

GINNI

"BABYMAMAMANIA"
Written by Pastor Jenn

Act 1, Scene 1
Stage Manager # 1 and #2 appear carrying applause/boo signs.

STAGE MANAGER #1
Welcome one and all to the Maury Show! I am one of your Stage Managers and we want to welcome you to today's last taping of the Maury show! Go Maury, Go Maury.

Both Stage Managers encourages crowd to chant "Go Maury" as if at a pep rally.

STAGE MANAGER #2
Ladies and gentlemen, the morning show was off the hook! Look, we had a pastor's wife bring her husband's ex-wife on the show to confront her about allegation's about an affair *and* a DNA test too! Then when it was proven that the pastor *was* the baby daddy ... Oh man, I felt so sorry for that poor lady!

STAGE MANAGER #1
Well, how about the other guests – Tonya, Sean and his mama! Uhm, Uhm, Uhm. It's a shame how women come on the show and can't get it through their thick heads that the man just don't want them. I mean, no matter how bad he treats her....

**STAGE MANAGER #1 &
STAGE MANAGER #2 (in unison)**
They still want to be with him!

STAGE MANAGER #2
But that Tonya from the morning taping
had it bad for that boy…she just couldn't
accept it was over between them.

STAGE MANAGER #1
Well I am sure, today's final taping of
our show will have as much if not more
drama for you, the Maury studio
audience. So, go ahead and give
yourselves a round of applause for being
here today!

Both Stage Managers encourages crowd to applaud

STAGE MANAGER #1
Now, in order to entice the home
audience to stay tuned to the Maury
Show, on occasion we will direct you to
respond in a certain way to certain
guests. When it is necessary for the
movement of our guests' stories, we will
indicate to you all when it is time to
applaud or boo. So let's try this together.

*Both Stage Managers lift the "CLAP" signs
and leads audience into a round of applause.*

STAGE MANAGER #2
Good. Now, let's practice the boos!

Both Stage Managers flip to the "BOO" sign, leading audience in an animated round of boos.

STAGE MANAGER #2

We have a good crowd tonight! With that said, please put your cell phones on vibrate and no texting…no talking…no twittering and no tweeting while we are taping. Matter of fact, just turn them off because there is nothing more irritating than having to sit next to you while you trying to *conversay!*

STAGE MANAGER #1

Now for those that brought your video cameras, let me take a moment here and help you all out. This is directed to those of you that are capturing the show on video for more than posterity's sake… We at the Maury Show have no problem with you wanting to tape your loved ones, but to then take your copies and sell them…

STAGE MANAGER #2

I got this! Bootleg is stolen property people! How you got the nerve to mass produce your own copies of someone else's blood, sweat and tears…. Most of the time you got people walking all across in front of the screen… your secret camera man laughing along with the jokes… Then you talking about "It play good, though"!

79

STAGE MANAGER #1

Look, if you got to get your hustle on anyway and bootleg our show, can you at least make sure you get a decent copy of it to Steve Harvey, Oprah and Tyler! And for you **Christians** that sell your soul for 5 DVDs for $20, shame on you, that's all I got to say... shame, shame, shame!

Stage Manager #1 points at audience in an accusatory manner

STAGE MANAGER #2

Lastly, as an advance warning, our cameras do pan the studio audience frequently, so if your face can be found on America's Most Wanted, you might want to creep out when the lights go down.

Stage Manager #2 scans the crowd as if looking for criminals. Suddenly, a crying Tonya enters from "Green Room" door, very upset with golden envelope in hand;

STAGE MANAGER # 1

Excuse me, Tonya, right? We showcased your story in the morning taping! What are you still doing here?

Sean enters onstage from "Green Room".

SEAN

I told you that wasn't my baby! I told you! Tonya, you know I got back with you for just for that one night, cause' you was beggin' me like you always do…just like you was beggin' me last night…

STAGE MANAGER #2

Look, you two are interrupting this taping! You had your chance earlier today!

Both Tonya and Sean ignore the Stage Managers.

TONYA

I'm sorry, Sean.

SEAN

Why you cryin' now… You wasn't cryin' when you had all them people booin' me on stage this morning cause they thought I was some punk for not takin' care of all your kids.

STAGE MANAGER #1

Both of you already had your 15 minutes of fame. You need to carry this on out of here!

TONYA

I'm so sorry…

SEAN

You only wanted me to be the baby daddy 'cause you still in love with me…

TONYA

I know, I know…. I thought it was you. I am really sorry!

STAGE MANAGER #2

Yea, she sorry alright!

SEAN

I takes care of mine, but I ain't payin' for or raisin' nobody else's kid. What you need to do is wipe your face and go and find your real baby daddy!

TONYA

I said I was sorry!

SEAN

See, you knew I was willing to man up if Shawnisha was mine too, that's why I brought you here. I needed my mama to know the truth!

Diane enters and runs directly to Tonya.

STAGE MANAGER #2

Not the mama too!

Both Stage Managers throw hands in the air and take seats on the stage to allow scene to play out.

DIANE

How could you play me like that! You knew all along you was with someone else; actin' like Sean was the only one!

TONYA
Mama Diane....

DIANE
Don't Mama me! You know I ain't got that much money, and you seen me down to my last but I still help you with them grandbabies. Now I come to find out that one of them ain't even mine....Oooh girl, You better be glad I am a Christian woman because if I wasn't... Lord help both of us! (***Looking up***) No, Lord help me!

SEAN
I told you she wasn't mine!

DIANE
Sean, Tonya told me it was your baby and I believed her. I stepped in only because you was mistreatin' baby girl.

SEAN
But that ain't my baby!

DIANE
That don't matter, she just a baby. That's they little sister and she only knows you as daddy! Don't treat her different, son!

SEAN
Nah, don't call me son. *That's* your daughter, I ain't yo' son. You the one that took her side... Mama, how come you didn't believe me!

DIANE

She look just like them other kids. How was I supposed to know?

Sean turns his attention angrily towards Tonya

SEAN

I knew, that's why we here! Tonya, I want you out of my life for good! I will continue to pay for *my* kids and pick up *my* boys. You can keep other dudes baby with you when I come by for mine.

TONYA

But you cain't leave 'cause we have other kids together. I never can say goodbye.

DIANE

(*Pleading*) No son... don't do that, please. Think about what that's gonna do to them kids.

SEAN

That's what you should'a been doin' Mama out there on that stage... thinkin' about *your* kid

DIANE

I am so sorry son; she told me this was your daughter too. How was I supposed to know she been with someone else?

Sean begins to cry openly as Stage Manager #1 feels compelled to comment on the situation.

STAGE MANAGER #1

Sean, in your mother's defense, we all believed Tonya. She had your mother and the entire studio audience this morning completely fooled.

Stage Manager #2 joins in the conversation.

STAGE MANAGER #2

Man, she even got me and I am usually on point with guests like her!

Sean wipes away his tears, looking at Diane

SEAN

You pierced me right to the core, Mama.

DIANE

Can you forgive me….

Sean does not respond, shaking his head in disappointment.

DIANE

Talk to me son…

Sean cannot answer, broken in spirit.

DIANE

Sean… Sean, baby I'm sorry I hurt you.

Diane turns her attention to Tonya angrily.

DIANE

You know, girl… God don't like ugly.
You sho' betta' be glad that the Lord
is merciful!

*Diane exits as Stage Manager #1 shows genuine
concern for the broken Sean.*

STAGE MANAGER #1

Ok son, now that your mother has left,
can the two of you take this back to the
Green Room? We really are behind
schedule for our taping.

Tonya goes over to Sean.

TONYA

Come on Sean, let's go to the Green
Room and talk things over… come on,
baby. Please, baby… please!

Sean snaps in anger, snatching away from Tonya.

SEAN

Nah, don't call me baby.. you need to
callin' you other baby daddy right about
now… .man… you knew all along that
wasn't my kid!

TONYA

Please forgive me, Sean… now that the
truth is out, can you give me another
chance? *Please* Sean, *please… please!*

SEAN

You triflin'!. You probably don't even know where you other baby daddy is!

TONYA

I just knew you was gonna be with me if Shawnisha was your baby too… Anyway… any *real* woman would try to keep her family together.

SEAN

Any *real* woman would know who the fathers of her children are!… That's what you get, messing around with two men at the same time!

TONYA

Men and their double standards!

SEAN

Whatever! That's just pathetic, begging to be with me again.

TONYA

So what, I did beg you to come and be with me 'cause I didn't want to alone on my birthday. You coulda said no! And, yea I started messing around with this other guy when you stopped taking my calls. That's why when I got pregnant, I wasn't sure who the father was.

SEAN

Like I said,… pathetic! You was the one lookin' stupid in front of the whole world on the Maury Show this morning!

TONYA
Stupid… Oh, I won't be the only one lookin' stupid if you gotta come back for another DNA test… I was hoping it *was* you. I still love you and I always will. No ring on her finger can change that. I am never gonna let you go!

SEAN
Oh, I'm not worried about you at all, Tonya!. And don't think I'ma gonna come runnin' when you call on your next birthday,…. You gonna keep callin' keep textin' and I'm gonna keep ballin' and keep flexin'!

Sean exits stage-right followed by Tonya who adlibs on the way off stage.

STAGE MANAGER #1
As you can see, there is never a dull moment on the Maury Show! Now that's out the way…. ladies and gentlemen, the stories you are about to hear are true!

STAGE MANAGER #2
However outlandish the behaviors, all the story line are real! You can't make this stuff up! Only the names have been changed to protect the ignorant!

STAGE MANAGER #1

Ladies and gentlemen, lets *finally* welcome Ashely to the stage!

Both Stage Managers lift the "CLAP" signs, taking seats on the opposite ends of the stage.

END SCENE 1

Act 1, Scene 2

Ashley enters pacing back and forth across stage; goes over to photo board. Bridgett follows Ashley onstage and takes a seat on the stage.

ASHLEY
Look at them,! they have the same eyes and the same nose.

Ashley points at pictures of Malik and the baby.

ASHLEY
Look, look at their ears (etc,)

At the actor's discretion, Ashley points out body parts; Ashley returns back to seat.

ASHLEY
Bring them out Maury... I am 200 % sure Malik is the father! Bring them out!

Stage Managers lift "CLAP" signs. Ashley moves two of the chairs over to opposite side of stage; Margarita enters alone.

ASHLEY
Where's Malik? Where's your son!

Stage Managers lift "BOO" signs

MARGARITA
I told him to wait backstage because I wanted to talk to you alone first. And I

am glad there are two of you here. Both
of you need to hear what I have to say!

*Margarita sits down on the chair, and positions
herself to deliver her speech.*

ASHLEY
Say what you gotta say, Miss Margarita,
you the one that brought me here.

MARGARITA
I am not going to let some young head
from the ghetto ruin my son's future!
Malik is destined for greatness! He has
pro scouts *lined* up to talk to him and the
last thing he needs right now is some
hood-rat holding him back!

*Bridgett and Ashley rise from their chairs in
response to derogatory remark immediately.*

BRIDGETT
Hood Rat!?!

ASHLEY
Excuse me!

*Stagehands intercept Bridgett preparing to attack
Margarita. Margarita reacts in a defensive
mannerism.*

MARGARITA
Why is it that you young Black women
today have lost your minds behind these
boys?! Don't you know that they will

toss your youthful innocence out like yesterday's trash! You think they love you; they don't! The only one who truly loves you is God.

ASHLEY
You don't know what you are talkin' about. And the Maury Show ain't no church either!

MARGARITA
God's church is everywhere! Let me tell you something, if a young man really loved you, he would honor God, you *and* your parents by waiting to be with you until you were married.

ASHLEY
You don't know nothin' about us.

MARGARITA
But I do know "suhin' about you. Actually I feel sorry for you.

Margarita rises from chair, moves toward edge of stage and addresses the audience.

MARGARITA
I have heard the horrible stories of Ashley's past. How she has slept with almost all the boys in the neighborhood and has no remorse about her actions! She is definitely not Rebecca of Sunny Brook Farms.

92

BRIDGETT
Rebecca who?

Ashley rises from chair to defend herself to the audience.

ASHLEY
I was wild, and I do regret it. But I stopped drinking and doing drugs the day I took the pregnancy test.

Both Stage Managers lift "CLAP" signs

ASHLEY
You can just ask Malik for yourself!

MARGARITA
You are not going to drag my son into this. I am tired of all your lies.

ASHLEY
It's your son that's the liar!

MARGARITA
My son is a strong Christian young man! He's our youth minister…. he teaches Sunday School.

BRIDGETT
That's not the only thing he teachin'!

MARGARITA
I am assuming you are a baby mama too!

BRIDGETT

What dat got to do with any thing? And hey, who's Rebecca?

MARGARITA

Look, this child looks nothing like my son.

Margarita rises and goes over to pictures; points at pictures to compare body parts while engaging the audience.

MARGARITA

Ashley, you are just trying my trap son! I don't want to have his dreams ruined.

ASHLEY

You need to bring him out here so we can talk about real dreams ruined.

Both Stage Managers lift "Boo" signs; Malik enters responding to boos; Ashley rushes to Malik in confrontation.

ASHLEY
You are such a liar!

BRIDGETT
A liar and a dog!

MALIK

Bridgett, what you doing here, this does not have anything to do with you.

BRIDGETT
She my girl, and I got her back!

MALIK
I would never bewith a woman unless she was my wife. What kind of Christian would I be then?

BRIDGETT
Just like most of them.

ASHLEY
If you never was with me, then why when we alone, you say you glad to be David's father? You say you want to marry me…

MARGARITA
Marry that! Uh uh.. I don't think so; not over my dead body.

Ashley points toward audience.

ASHLEY
But your mother told those people out there that she heard stories of how I used to sleep around…. like I never changed. Tell her the truth Malik!

MALIK
The truth is that I can't be the father because I am a virgin, and very proud of that fact!. So why would you want to pin this baby on me? All I have been to you

is a good friend, Ashley. Why would
you do this to me?

ASHLEY
Do this to you... look watcha doin' to
me!

MALIK
Ashley, even my own family says that
the kid does not look like me.

Malik rises and goes over to the pictures.

MALIK
Look at him, he don't look like me...
Look at his hair, his eyes, his ears...

MARGARITA
I told you that ghetto hood rat is trying
to ruin your reputation!

ASHLEY
Look, I ain't gonna be too many more
hood rats....I can't believe this....

*Ashley cries softly into her hands; Bridgett
comforts her friend.*

BRIDGETT
I can.

Malik sits, trying to convince Margarita.

MALIK

But I tried to help her, Mother. I told her I could *only* be her friend. She knows she a roller and everybody else knows she a roller. It is what it is!

Ashley rises from chair, hysterically addressing the audience.

ASHLEY

It is not fair Malik gets to live free and I gotta miss out on life! I cain't go to parties, I had to quit school. It's hard being a single mother…

MARGARITA

Well, you should have kept your legs closed. The reckless, pitiful.. disgusting life you have has nothing to do with my son! He is not your child's father!

Ashley approaches Margarita to prove her point, Margarita over reacts, Stagehands intercept.

ASHLEY

You were not there! You didn't lay in the bed with me, Malik did!

Ashley turns to the audience to gain support.

ASHLEY

She's the reason my son has no father. Let me tell you what she did! My son was a premie, he only weighed 1 lb 4 oz.

The doctors told me he wasn't gonna live past his first birthday!

MARGARITA
That's not my son's baby.

Ashley ignores Margarita and continues talking to audience.
ASHLEY
I had to go over 200 times to the hospital *without* my son's daddy because Malik's mama wouldn't let him come!

Both Stage Managers lift the "BOO" signs.

MARGARITA
That's right, because that's *not* my son's baby!

Ashley turns attention back to Margarita.

ASHLEY
But he is grown! Malik is *way* over 18. You won't even let your grown son be a father to his own baby!

Margarita approaches Ashley in menacing way.

MARGARITA
What I won't do is let you or a sick baby risk my son's future! I have worked too hard to ensure his success. So, how could I let him get emotionally attached to this child especially since it is not his. For what would happen when that sick

baby finally passed away? My son would have been so distraught and that could jeopardize his chances for a pro football career. It is *still* my responsibility to shelter him from situations like this and girls like you!

Ashley collapses back into the chairs, crying; Bridgett rises to comfort her.

BRIDGETT
Hey, Malik's mama…..what you gonna do if he is the father?

MARGARITA
I will tell you this, if Malik is the father, the first thing I will do is pop him up-side his head for being so careless! Then I will make *sure* my son does the right thing to support his child. But I am not worried about that, because my son does not lie to me, our relationship is based on trust and respect. So if he said that's not his child, then that's not his child.

Bridgett rises from seat, gesturing towards Malik and addresses the audience

BRIDGETT
To all the teen girls out in the audience, take a good look at this piece of trash, yall need watch out for this boy! His name is Malik Ivory Jefferson…run when you see him comin! He thinks he a

man, but he ain't. Look what he doin' to
my girl!

MALIK
You better watch your mouth!

Bridgett lunges at Malik who is startled, being caught off guard; finishes addressing audience.

BRIDGETT
Malik gonna sweet talk ya, get what he
want then he don't know you no more…
I know that for myself cause he the
father of my baby too!

Ashley abruptly stops crying; Margarita responds as if she doesn't believe the allegation; Malik responds in denial to the statement.

ASHLEY
What!!!

Bridgett pleads for forgiveness from Ashley.

BRIDGETT
Ashley, I am so sorry. I came here today
to reveal my secret that I been sleeping
with Malik too and that he is the father
of my son.

Ashley violently breaks the embrace and grabs Bridgett who motions towards stagehands for help; Stagehands act as if they don't see anything.

ASHLEY

All this time, you been sleepin' with him! I tell you everything about us! How you gonna do me like this ….

Malik rises from his seat and breaks the girls up, he become "ghetto"

MALIK

See, yall know I'm goin' pro, so yall trying to trap me off! The rest of them cats don't have nothin' goin' for them, they not trying to get out the game, I am.

Malik returns to his seat with attitude.

MALIK

Ain't one of yall ain't got enough woman to keeps me down!

Margarita slaps Malik on the head.

MARGARITA

Malik, when did you start talking Ghetto?

Bridgett tries to convince Ashley regarding Malik.

BRIDGETT

Remember the night you first was with Malik at the youth retreat,

MARGARITA

At the *youth* retreat…

MALIK

Mother, she is lying. I never was with either of them! You have to believe me!

BRIDGETT

Ashley, Malik told you, the same thing he told me when he left my tent.

.

ASHLEY

What are you talkin' about!

BRIDGETT

You know how he says that Jesus loves you?

ASHLEY

He always says that. So what!

BRIDGETT

But does he always say that Jesus loves you *anyway*…

Bridgett and Ashley say rest of sentence together.

BRIDGETT & ASHLEY

… and *anyhow*.

Ashley collapses to the stage floor, broken.

ASHLEY

Oh my God, Lord Help me! Oooohhh nooooooo!

Margarita, for the first time, shows nervousness.

MARGARITA
Well that does not prove anything!

BRIDGETT
Then how come I know he got a star-shaped birthmark on his left butt cheek?

Margarita quickly stands up, rolls up her sleeves.

MARGARITA
Oh, I am about to go to jail!

Margarita stands up, rolls up sleeves on and acts like she is going to attach Bridgett but turns to attack Malik; Malik tries to fend off punches; Stagehands step in to break them up and assist Ashley back to her chair.

BRIDGETT
I don't care what your mama says, Malik when the test come back that you is my baby's father, you gonna step up and help me take care of this baby, too. Knowin' you, you probably got a baby with that Rebecca chick too yo mama was talkin' bout.

Bridgett stands up and addresses audience.

BRIDGETT
Come on, bring them results, We all want to know the truth right, … read 'em right now!

While Narrator reads the results from off stage, Bridgett speaks along with announcer.

NARRATOR
In the case of 8-month-old James,..

NARRATOR & BRIDGETT (in unison)
Malik you are.... ....

NARRATOR
NOT the father!

BRIDGETT
OH MY GOD!!

Bridgett runs off the stage, screaming..

MALIK
See, I told you! I knew that wasn't my baby. Thank you Jesus for the truth!

Malik turns attention to Ashley.

MALIK
And when your son's results come back too, that I am NOT the father, Ashley, I cannot be your friend any longer.... don't call me, don't text me, don't even mention my name!

Ashley tries to hug Malik amid tearful pleas; Malik pushes her away and returns to chair.

ASHLEY

You said you loved me, Malik. You said
you wanted to marry me and be a father
to our son! Why, Malik… Why…

*Ashley slumps back into her seat; Margarita
embraces Malik's shoulders.*

MARGARITA

Look it has already been proven that
these girls are lying on my son. So let's
hear those results and be done with all
this mess… I've got better things to do
with my time than to be sitting here on
the Maury Show with all this mayhem
and foolishness!

NARRATOR

In the case of 6-month-old David ……
Malik you ARE the father!

*Stage Manager #2 lifts the "CLAP" sign as
Malik exits crying out of control, others adlib
in character. Before exiting with her son,
Margarita slaps Malik on the head.*

STAGE MANAGER #1
Excuse me Ashley, are you a Christian?

ASHLEY
I thought I was… until today…

STAGE MANAGER #1

Here take this envelope... There's a church across the street that has help for you concerning your son.

Stage Manger tries to give Ashley the golden envelope; she refuses it.

ASHLEY

The church.... Humph, you seen what the "church" just done *to* me!

STAGE MANAGER #1

Don't mind him... I want you to go on over there and get that help...

ASHLEY

I know you tryin' to help, but the church *cain't* do nothin' for me or my son! So...you know what, you can keep your envelope and you can keep your Jesus!

Ashley exits as Stage Manager #1 calls to her.

STAGE MANAGER #1

Good luck, dear-heart... and God Bless!

STAGE MANAGER #2

Let's change the mood a bit...We have a special treat for you all as we provide live musical entertainment for our studio audience during the commercial breaks.

STAGE MANAGER #1

That's right! Ladies and gentlemen, the Motown Review Tour is here in the Maury studio!

STAGE MANAGER #2

Our first guests headed up one of the most powerful live acts on the R&B circuit during the '60s and early '70s!

STAGE MANAGER #1

They specialized in a funked-up combination of soul and rock that few R&B acts could hope to match!

STAGE MANAGER #2

In 1971, they won the Grammy for the Best R&B Group...

STAGE MANAGER #1
STAGE MANAGER #2 (in unison)

Let's give it up ladies and gentlemen for Ike and Tina Turner!

Both Stage Managers lift "CLAP" signs as lip syncers/ dancers take the stage to perform;

END SCENE 2

Act 1, Scene 3

STAGE MANAGER #1
Let's give it up once again for Ike &
Tina Turner

*Both Stage Managers pump the crowd about the
last performance.*

STAGE MANAGER #2
Let's welcome our next guest to the stage!

*Both Stage Managers lift the "CLAP" signs, as
Daryl enters with a heavy heart, plopping down in
the chair.*

DARYL
I cannot believe I am sitting on the
Maury show trying to prove to my wife
that I am the father of my own baby.
Bring her out!

*Both Stage Managers lift "BOO" signs as
Anne enters and goes over to chair, moving hers
away from his.*

ANNE
Daryl, you know you are not my baby's
father!

*Anne turns to address the audience to challenge
Daryl's claim.*

ANNE
He got you all believing his sob story! I
am a gazillion percent sure Daryl is not

the father! Look at him; he is too old to make any kids!

DARYL

You only come around me just to pick up what you need. I give you all my money.... I know... I know I'm just a fool in love with you!

ANNE

It wasn't like you didn't know what you was gettin' when you married me in the first place. You wanted to give me everything so I took it. All you needed me to do was to marry you.

DARYL

Yea, but when I married you, I finally thought I caught you and your love was mine... all mine, baby girl.

ANNE

Ok, I thought I could deal with it but after awhile, your old behind started looking really old.... My son looks just like your nephew anyway.

DARYL

I know that boy is mine... I know that with all my heart, my soul and my strength! Look at him, doesn't he look like me!

109

Both Stage Managers lift the "CLAP" signs as Daryl goes to photo and points to body parts etc.

DARYL
We have the same forehead, the same ears!

ANNE
Ray Charles can even see that my baby don't even look like this dude.

Daryl looks toward Stage Manager #1; pointing toward the photos.

DARYL
Hey, Stage Manager!

Stage Manager appears on stage and listens to question in character.

STAGE MANAGER #1
You do know we are taping right?

DARYL
Can you show the back of the baby's head? I have a peanut head and her head is flat. My son has the same peanut shape.

ANNE
Man, you sound like a fool.

State Manager #1 & Daryl return to seats.

DARYL

I might sound like a fool, but I made up my mind, I'm gonna be your sugar daddy, your baby daddy and any other kind of daddy you need.

ANNE

I don't need you to be nothin' to me or my son. I know who the father is. But if you want to keep giving me your money anyway, I'ma take it.

Daryl rises from his seat and addresses the audience to plead his case.

DARYL

Do you know my wife would make me crawl for her love?

ANNE

You need to crawl your old behind back home because he is not your son.

Both Stage Managers lift the "BOO" signs. As audience responds accordingly, Anne argues with crowd.

ANNE

So what? And...and. .. that's right, I took his money... yall don't know me etc, etc..

Anne turns her attention back to Daryl.

ANNE

Man, you trippin', you know that's not your baby! You even put my son's picture on your facebook page!

DARYL

That's the only way I can even see my son. Why are you doing this to me? You know I thought I would never have kids, now that God has answered my prayer, you want to deny *me* visitation.

Both Stage Managers lift the "BOO" signs.

ANNE

I deny you visitation because it's not your baby!

Anne addresses the audience, responding to boos.

ANNE

Whatever.... Yall' don't know me... I know who the father of my baby is!

Daryl continues to address the audience, becoming progressively angrier.

DARYL

So many Black men don't even acknowledge their children, and if they do, very few of them actually take care of them financially, physically and emotionally....

Daryl aggressively lunges at Anne and Stage hands hold him back while Anne acts like she wants to fight him back.

DARYL

Yet, you won't let me care for my own! Even after I caught you in bed with my nephew! I was still there through the pregnancy, not my nephew... It was me! I was there when my son was born! I been taking care of him ever since! And I will still take care of him even if is not mine!

ANNE

I don't need you to take care of him, because he is not your baby! Your nephew should be here, not you!

Daryl's mood changes to a contained anger as he returns to his seat.

DARYL

I told that boy that he better not show up here! He was like a son to me, so I know that he can *never* fix what has been broken in trust between us. I just want to know why me, why he picked my wife... why did he do it?

Daryl looks heartfelt over at Anne; Daryl begins to cry.

DARYL
Anne...why did you do it?

C.K.SHA' rises from the audience seat and blurts out response.

C.K. SHA'

Cause she's a home wrecker!… That's right, I said it…she's a home wrecker!

Both Stage Managers lift the "CLAP" signs as Anne moves across stage to confront C.K. Sha'

ANNE

Little girl, you betta watch yourself!

C.K. SHA'

Why you let her get to you like this, Uncle Daryl? She ain't worth it! She don't care nothin' about you, she don't care nothin' about none of us!

ANNE

You need to sit yourself back down in that seat and mind your own business!

C.K. Sha' shows great rage directed toward Anne.

C.K. SHA'

I hate you, Anne! I wish you was never in our family. You done messed everything up. My brother is gone and he probably ain't never commin' back!

ANNE

Like I said, this is grown folks business. Mind your own!

C.K. Sha' leaves her seat, arguing with Anne as she makes her way onstage.

C.K. SHA'
You make it my business when I gotta hear my uncle cryin' bout what you and my brother did. He was all I had left after my mama left us!

C.K. Sha' points toward Daryl.

C.K. SHA'
You had a husband, but that wasn't good enough, was it! You just had to go after my brother too! Didn't you!

ANNE
You need to shut up. C... K....Sha'... What kind of Ghetto name is that anyway? I bet yo' mama named you after her favorite cologne, huh?

C.K. Sha' rushes at Anne, who doesn't flinch" Stage hands grab her and sets her down in a chair.

C.K. SHA'
Keep makin' fun of my name! You gonna get hurt!

DARYL
Anne, what is wrong with you! She's just a kid! Don't you have any remorse for what you did?

C.K. SHA' shows rage; breaks down, crying.

DARYL

C.K. SHA', you don't need to talk about this, especially on TV ….

C.K. SHA'

No, I want her to know what she did, and I don't care who knows.

C.K. Sha' approaches Anne, wiping her tears and, getting up in Anne's face.

C.K. SHA'

I cain't understand why my brother would hurt our uncle like that? I asked him why did he do it and he told me you was all up in his face and he wasn't strong enough to keep tellin' you no.

Anne pushes C.K. Sha's face away from hers.

ANNE

Oh, your brother didn't tell you about the hundred dollar bill he had in his hand while he was hollarin' "NO" right? It was nothin' personal; it was just business… anyway…Daryl, you knew what I was when you married me.

C.K. SHA'

Even I knew what you was when he married you… I told my uncle not to marry you! I knew you was fake with all that Church talk!

116

ANNE

Whateva'! I don't have to explain anything I do to some child! I am grown! Shut up! Don't you try and preach to me little girl!

C.K. SHA'

I knew you was gonna do somethin' like this…. You just like my momma!

C.K. Sha' returns to her chair in tears as Daryl confronts Anne, moved to tears as well.

DARYL

Do you see what your choices have brought about!? I took care of that boy like he was my own…I put him through school… put clothes on his back, money in his pocket and look how he repaid me… he slept with my wife and now look where we are …

Anne starts to shows signs of remorse

ANNE

Daryl, I'm sorry … I really am trying to get myself together… you know I done started goin' to back to church… gave my life to Christ all over again …but it seems like its too late to change some things…

C.K. Sha' shouts at Anne in the midst of her tears.

117

C.K. SHA'

You finally said somethin' right! It is too late… you ain't never gonna change!

DARYL

All I have ever wanted was to be a father….don't get me wrong…taking care of my niece and nephew filled that void, in my life.. but when my son was born… when I held him in my arms for the first time… I knew there was a God!

Anne is visibly bothered by C.K.Sha's remark while continuing to address Daryl.

ANNE

Look, I know who the father of my son is; I have no doubt… Your nephew is so shame for what he did to you, he took off and we all know he will make sure we won't ever be able to find him….so that means that my son will never know his father…. Just read the results so I can get off this stage!

Narrator's voice is heard from offstage; C.K. SHA' grabs Daryl's hand in support in anticipation for the results; both Stage Managers show anticipation for a good outcome for Daryl.

NARRATOR

When it comes to the case of 3 month – year-old Gregory, Daryl you are….

Daryl responds prematurely as if he is the father because of the Narrator's pause.

NARRATOR
…. NOT the father!

Daryl crumbles; C.K.Sha' tries to console Daryl. Both Stage Managers react with utter disappointment.

C.K. SHA'
That's okay, Uncle Daryl. You don't need her anyway… She is not worth it!

ANNE
I told you Gregory wasn't your son!

Anne addresses the audience one last time in a more subdued manner, showing remorse.

ANNE
I told him…. I told him he wasn't the father. He didn't want to believe me.

C.K. SHA' with the help of Stagehands lift Daryl from the floor.

C.K. SHA'
Come on Uncle Daryl… let's go home… you don't have to cry no more… it's over… it's finally over!

Anne exits as Stage Manager #1 reluctantly hands her a golden envelope.

STAGE MANAGER #2
Wow!… all I can say is wow!

STAGE MANAGER #1
And I was really pulling for Daryl. I was hoping that the baby was his…

STAGE MANAGER #2
Wow!

STAGE MANAGER #1
Ok, ladies and gentlemen, as you can see, even we get caught up in the story lines…. Well, we've got to go on with the show.

STAGE MANAGER #2
Our next special guests from the Motown Review Tour were the most successful American performers of the 1960s in terms of red-hot commercial appeal!

STAGE MANAGER #1
They reeled off five number one singles in a row from 1964-65!

STAGE MANAGER #2
You all know their #1 songs! "Where Did Our Love Go"

STAGE MANAGER #1
"Baby Love,"

STAGE MANAGER #2
"Come See About Me,"

120

STAGE MANAGER #1
"Back in My Arms Again"

STAGE MANAGER #2
And here tonight, performing for you,
"Stop! In the Name of Love,"

STAGE MANAGER #1 & # 2
Ladies and gentlemen, welcome to the
stage Diana Ross & the Supremes!

*Both Stage Managers lift "CLAP" signs as lip
syncers/ dancers take the stage to perform*

END SCENE 3

Act 1, Scene 4

STAGE MANAGER #1

Lets give it up, one more time for Diana Ross & the Supremes!

Both Stage Managers pump the crowd about the last performance. Matthew enters goes straight to the pictures of the 3 men and the twins. Antoinette enters .

MATTHEW

This dude, Antoinette? This dude right here?

ANTOINETTE

Well at least Sean showed up, Freddie said he was tired of coming on TV... said I was making him look like a fool.

MATTHEW

No, I'm the one that looks like a fool! It's m*y* picture that is between two other men! I knew you had four baby daddies when I met you, but I didn't know you had been on the Maury Show and tested your ex-boyfriend Freddie (***pointing at picture***) each time for those kids.

ANTOINETTE

He sayin' he ain't the father of them neither.

MATTHEW

So you mean to tell me that even after all that, after he dogged you on national TV all four times you two have been on the show… you are still sleeping with him?

ANTOINETTE
I am sorry I hurt you, boo.. . I cain't help it, baby…

MATTHEW
Man, you could have told me about that Sean dude when we saw him in the green room. That is messed up!

Matthew sits in his chair with force. Antoinette begins to plead with Matthew.

ANTOINETTE
I didn't know how to tell you about sleepin' with him; you was already mad because I told you about me sleepin' with Freddie. It don't matter anyway…. you the one baby… you are the one! These are your kids…. Boy, you know that baby girl looks just like you!

MATTHEW
What do you mean I am the one? You just told me a couple of days ago that you was with someone else and the twins might not be mine. Now today, you are convinced I am the father. You expect me to just overlook this, just forget my wife is wicked! I don't know if I could ever trust you again.

ANTOINETTE
You can trust me, I promise…

Both Stage Managers lift the "BOO" signs.. Antoinette rises from seat to argue with crowd.

ANTOINETTE
Shut up… you don't know me.. Whatever….(etc)

Antoinette turns attention back to Matthew.

ANTOINETTE
Matthew, I never meant to hurt you, but I needed for us to find out the truth. I promise I won't do it no more. I'm sorry.

MATTHEW
Nah… you beyond sorry!

ANTOINETTE
Please forgive me baby…It was a mistake.

MATTHEW
Aren't you tired of coming on the Maury show?

Matthew begins to cry; works to hold back tears.

MATTHEW
If you loved me Antoinette… really loved me…, you wouldn't keep making mistakes like this, because it is not a mistake after the first time.

Matthew walks over to Antoinette to remove wedding ring from her finger.

MATTHEW

I should have done this the other day, when I had to let some stranger swab my mouth to see if I am the father to my own children! (*To audience holding up the ring*)All you men in the studio audience, when you see my wife Antoinette hanging out... think twice. She is not worth the trouble.

Matthew turns his attention back to Antoinette as he puts the ring into his pocket.

MATTHEW

Do you realize that you put my life at risk?! What the ....

Matthew catches himself before cursing; he takes his seat in defeat.

MATTHEW

What is wrong with you!

Antoinette she retakes her seat.

ANTOINETTE

I don't know what's wrong with me; I guess I'm just addicted!

MATTHEW

Ok, so now you're trying to sound like Tiger Woods.

ANTOINETTE

No really, I *am* addicted. I got the same disease he got, just like what them White doctors was talkin' bout on TV.

MATTHEW

No… you just nasty!

Both Stage Managers lift "CLAP" signs, Antoinette begins to argue crowd.

ANTOINETTE

Whateva'… yall don't know me… etc.

MATTHEW

Let me tell you something, I get tired of grown men trying to blame their whorish ways on some convenient, new age terminology. Being with a bunch of people is not a disease; it is sin. Period! Dudes like Tiger Woods need to quit punkin' out with that sorry excuse, like it's a real disease. Look at him, he had a wife… beautiful children, money, but he still was not satisfied.

Antoinette tries to embrace Matthew.

ANTOINETTE

But, I am satisfied with you baby.

MATTHEW

Nah, you confused! Look at you…

Mathew rises and returns to the 3 pictures.

MATTHEW

You got Freddie who wants to prove he
is *not* the father again, you got me here
because I want to prove I *am* the father,
and then you got this dude Sean who
kept telling me all he wants to know is *if*
he is the father. I thought he was talking
about his own baby mama drama… not
talking about my wife too.

*Sean enters from "Green Room" Matthew stands
up but does not approach Sean; Antoinette smiles.*

SEAN

Hey brotha, I'm sorry, I had no idea this
chick was your wife. I didn't even know
she was married when I met her on the
corner. When she told me I might be the
father of her twins, since I was comin'
here already for my own situation, the
Stage Managers put us on together. I
didn't know that she didn't tell you
about me, man. I thought you knew.

MATTHEW

Well, as you can see, my wife likes to
keep secrets.

Antoinette speaks up sheepishly.

ANTOINETTE

I do have another secret, Matthew…

127

MATTHEW
Oh Lord! Now what... the Stagehands might be the twins' father too?

One Stagehand adlibs angrily at the accusation; One looks guilty.

ANTOINETTE
Matthew, I'm pregnant.

All respond in unison and react in character

MATTHEW, STAGE MANAGER #1 , STAGE MANAGER #2 & STAGE HANDS (in unison)
You're pregnant?!

Sean shows immediate agitation.

SEAN
Check this, it cain't be me, bro. We only was together that one time. She was too out there for me. Man, you good... I don't know how you do it! Stay married to this one!

MATTHEW
I *can't* do it any more! *(to Antoinette)* When I said for better or for worse, I had no idea you was going to push me to my limit. ... Antoinette, if these kids are not mine, I am leaving you!

Male Stagehands that reacted to the accusation grabs signs from the Stage Managers and lift the

128

"CLAP" sign; Antoinette argues with them and audience.; Antoinette then jumps onto Mathew

ANTOINETTE
How are you going to leave us, Matthew?

Matthew peels Antoinette off him

MATTHEW
I am not leaving them, Antoinette… I am leaving you! No matter what happens with the results, those are my kids and I will always be their father…but I need to know the truth for myself. I can't let them grow up like I had to… my father never came around… saying he couldn't find me.. We have the same name! We lived in the same neighborhood. How are you not going to know who I am!

Antoinette tries to seduce Matthew with her body.

ANTOINETTE
But how you gonna leave *this*, baby?

Both Matthew, Head Stagehand & Sean are mesmerized and pause in "Hear, Speak, See No Evil" stance; Sean speaks up nervously.

SEAN
Well…well.. uh.. uh.. I want you to know Antoinette, if they my kids, I will definitely man up.

ANTOINETTE

Shut up, Sean, ain't nobody even talking to you.

Tonya appears from "Green Room" Door

TONYA

Sean, how you gonna man up and you still live with your mama?

Tonya points at Antoinette.

TONYA

Who's that, Sean? Is this the Rebecca everybody talkin' about in the green room?

ANTOINETTE

Don't worry about who I am!

Tonya attempts to rush Antoinette prepared to tussle; the ladies square off in character; Stage hands do not intervene, supporting Tonya.

MATTHEW

Stop it!!! Antoinette, I thought you said you're pregnant!

Antoinette reacts in a very pregnant state, sits down in seat. Matthew looks toward heaven.

MATTHEW

God help me! Look just read the results. I can't take this any longer; I need to know. I just need to know....

TONYA

That's right I need to know too.. Go ahead and read them results!

NARRATOR

When it comes to the case of one-month-old twins, Samuel and Irene... Sean you are NOT the father.

Sean shows signs of over-exuberant joy; does a cartwheel across the stage and out the auditorium down center aisle; Tonya follows after him.

NARRATOR

In the case of one-month old Irene, Matthew you ARE the father!

ANTOINETTE

See baby, we can stay a family. I love you baby. We have another chance.

Antoinette motions for Matthew to return her ring He retrieves ring and begins to place ring on her finger as rest of results are read.

NARRATOR

When it comes to one-month-old Samuel, Matthew... you are NOT the father!

Matthew snatches ring off Antoinette's finger and exits; Antoinette begins to exit, Stage Manager #1 who makes no attempt to give an envelope to her.

ANTOINETTE

Why come I ain't getting' no envelope like the rest on the chicks.

STAGE MANAGER #1

Well, this is an opportunity to help *Christian* women with their children...

STAGE MANAGER #2

And as many times we have had you as guest here on the Maury show, we just figured you couldn't possible be one!

ANTOINETTE

Quit playin' , I been saved my whole life!

Antoinette snatches envelope from Stage Manager #1 and ; Stage hands exit.

STAGE MANAGER #1

Well, this concludes our final taping for today! Thanks for being a part of it all!

STAGE MANAGER #2

Before you go, however, we do have one more group from the Motown Review Tour to close out the Maury Show!

STAGE MANAGER #1

As the biggest phenomenon in pop music during the early '70s, Their first single "I Want You Back" hit number one on both the pop and R&B charts!

STAGE MANAGER #2
So did their second single, "ABC" !

STAGE MANAGER #1
The third single, "The Love You Save", certified them as pop sensations…

STAGE MANAGER #2
And the release of "I'll Be There," made them the first and only group in pop history to have their first four singles hit number one!

STAGE MANAGER #1
With out further ado, ladies and gentlemen help us welcome to the stage…

STAGE MANAGER #1 &#2 (in unison)
Michael, Marlon, Jermaine, Tito, & Jackie!…. The Jackson 5!

Lip syncers/dancers take the stage to perform.

END SCENE 4

Act 1, Scene 5

As Jackson 5 dancers leave the stage, both Stage Managers pack up to leave and actors reappear from the "Green Room", dressed in jackets as if heading home, exiting down center aisle, adlibbing in character in this order:

Tonya & Ashley
(Tonya talks re: Ashley's acceptance of envelope)

Sean & Diane
(Diane still apologizing, Tonya joins them)

Bridgett
(Ashley flees Bridgett, refusing her apology)

Anne
(Talking to God about her mistakes)

Margarita and Malik
(Margarita scolds Malik about his sin)

C.K.Sha' and Daryl
(C.K.Sha' comforts a numb Daryl)

Antoinette and Matthew
(Antoinette begging Matthew for a chance)

Stagehands and both Stage Managers
(Discussing the shows revelations)

As actors disperse, Yana enters crying.

YANA

Oh my God…..oh my God… Why… Why…. I have been your faithful servant Lord, I have been a good wife to him… now what about me..… what about me! Why does every man in my life have to cheat on me… What is up with your *man-of-God*… He can't control himself either…. He is just as bad if not worse than the men in the streets….

Ginni appears from "Green Room" fanning herself with a golden envelope, pointing the phone in Yana's direction.

YANA

He says he loves you Lord…… he says he loves me, but then he will do this to me… He supposed to love me like Christ loves the church… My husband is supposed to lay down his life for me! For me, Lord!

Yana crumbles to her knees and prays quietly but audibly under Ginni's phone conversation.

GINNI

Can you hear her???..... Yea…. That's just what she sounded like when the results came back saying that you were the father…. Talking about "Oh My God"…, like she didn't know....

Ginni circles around Yana, preparing to take a picture of the crying Yana.

GINNI

You should see her…. Yea….she crying like a fool… looking like a hot mess. . I told her I was going to get you back …. What?..... so…. I know you not feeling sorry for her, she's the one that brought *me* here……, It's her fault….. so now she knows the truth like the rest of world.

Ginni sees Yana wiping tears; both ladies prepare to confront each other.

GINNI

Look, let me call you back. I need to talk to wifey for a minute. …. What? …. Don't worry about what I am going to say to her… If she don't want to hear what I have to say, she shouldn't have brought me to the Maury show…. Ok…It's too late for all of that now… *I'll holla!*

Ginni hangs up the phone.

YANA

Just so you know Ginni, I brought you to the Maury Show because I needed to find out if all the text messages, voice mails, emails you keep sending my husband about him being the father of your baby were true.

GINNI

You *knew* the truth…You didn't have to bring me here, so you brought all this on yourself! It don't even matter that they were booing me out there on the stage, everybody saw you as stupid!

YANA

For some reason, he cannot get you out of his system. I have spent the better part of our marriage trying to live up to the ghosts of his past, namely you!

GINNI

There is no way you can ever live up to what I was able to give him.

YANA

Why couldn't you just leave us alone? We were happy together until you came back to church… You mean to tell me you could not have found any other place to worship?

GINNI

I am a grown woman… I can go where I want to go and I can do what I want to do.

YANA

I thought you didn't even want children, Ginni? He told me that's one of the reasons why your marriage failed.

GINNI

Well, that was before he became *famous*.

YANA

Is that all you do? Wait for those who have prestige? He told me how you seduced every man that came your way, thinking he could outdo the one you're with... never just satisfied with your life!

Ginni giggles in her own amusement.

GINNI

I am now... Yana honey, I have the stuff that he wants, I am the thing that he needs, not you!

YANA

Devil, I see you,.....You are so dirty!

GINNI

I might be dirty, but your husband likes this dirty dirty! Matter of fact, I just remembered I told him I was gonna call him back.

Ginni acts as if she is calling and being hung up on several times; Yana talks to God.

YANA

Lord, you know I've been here so many times before... At least with the other women, they weren't anything more to him than just casual flings...

Ginni angered due to failed phone call attempts.

GINNI
Hello... hello.... Oh! I know he didn't just hang up on me! Oh... ok!

YANA
But with you, it's different because I know at one point he loved you...

GINNI
He *still* loves me.

YANA
No he doesn't. How can he? He doesn't even love himself.

GINNI
And I am going to make sure he stands behind his promises for a glamorous life for both me and his daughter.

YANA
Do you really think my husband can promise you fortune and fame because of who he is? Do you think you will have a life that's so carefree because of his ministry? Once this news hits, there will be no more ministry, no more church, no more nothing!

GINNI
That's what you say...

Ginni makes phone call; agitated.

GINNI

Hello.. Pastor…you know I have been trying to call you…

Ginni reacts to phone call, as if she does not want to hear other party; Yana collapses, crying.

YANA

Oh my God, Father what am I going to do…. What will the church think about our Pastor having a love child with his ex… how will I live with the shame .. my husband unfaithful to me and his congregation…And Lord, I don't know if can deal with Ginni *today* of all people, not after all that has happened! How am I going to face her now…after all this, and still have to minister to her? How strong do you expect me to be Lord.. She slept with my husband… she has a child for him and now is planning on being with him… How strong do you need me to be all the time God? I know I have to forgive them… forgive her… But can I even face her today… tomorrow… or for the rest of my marriage is the real question. Lord… I just want to die right now…

Ginni yells into the phone; Yana slowly exits down center aisle.

GINNI

What do you mean I'll never make you stay?. Boy, you belong with me. I am

who you are supposed to be with, not
her. I am the one who gave you a baby,
not her! What! …. What you say… you
can't leave her… you love **her**… Nah…
I can't deal with this right now, I will
talk to you later when I get home.

*Ginni closes phone with force quickly follows
Yana down center aisle, yelling at Yana from
behind as both women ext.*

GINNI

I don't know what he sees in you
anyway! Talking about he's not going to
leave you for me... hoping that you will
forgive him…huh.. We gonna see about
that! You hear me Yana! We gonna see
about that!

END SCENE 5

END ACT 1

INTERMISSION

141

Act 2
Across the street from the Maury Show

Head Stagehand enters as women walk into auditorium; Antoinette, Ashley and Ginni are on opposite sides than Tonya and Anne.

HEAD STAGEHAND
Come on ladies. I need you to hurry on across the street …

TONYA
Hey, that's the bouncer guy from the Maury Show!

ANNE
They gave you guys an envelope too?

ASHLEY
Yea it looks like all of us got one.

TONYA
Did they tell yall somethin' bout some money?

GINNI
Yes, something like that.

ANTOINETTE
I wonder what it is. They said don't open it until you get across the street.

Tonya points at Antoinette and shakes her head.

TONYA
Girl… you nasty!

142

ANNE

Leave her alone, she is not worth your trouble!

ANTOINETTE

Don't be jealous 'cause Sean got some of this too!

TONYA

Everybody got some of that, so what that make you?

ASHLEY

Miss Antoinette, should just ignore her.

GINNI

I think that would be a good idea, girlfriend!

ANTOINETTE

Ha ha ha …..You just mad because he don't want you. I heard you cryin' backstage.

TONYA

Oh but you was cryin' and beggin' too...
Honey…. Give me another chance…

ANTOINETTE

You betta shut up!

ASHLEY

I don't think you wanna go there…

GINNI

Why don't you just ignore her like
Ashley said!

TONYA

And how your twins got different
daddies! Like I said… nasty!

GINNI

Different fathers? Really?… wow!

ANNE

Yea, that is nasty!

ANTOINETTE

I know you not talking, when you slept
with your husband's own nephew!

ASHLEY

Come on…just leave them alone so we
can just get across the street!

ANNE

Like I said on stage, it wasn't personal, it
was just business.

TONYA

Triflin'!

ANTOINETTE

What you say?

TONYA

You heard what I said… triflin'!

ANTOINETTE
You better be glad you over there!

ASHLEY
I don't think you need to be sayin'
nothin!   She look like she can fight!

TONYA
Why what you gonna do?

ANTOINETTE
I'ma show you what I'm gonna do!

Antoinette and Tonya walk toward each other,
arguing about the confrontation on stage earlier.

HEAD STAGEHAND
Hey… hey… no… no… Ladies, please.
No violence!

Antoinette reaches Tonya; they square up, face to
face; Antoinette touches her hips, waist etc.

ANTOINETTE
Sean wanted this… he don't want you!

TONYA
I am tired of you gettin' in my face!

Ashley walks past Antoinette and Tonya.

ASHLEY
Really, all yall need to quit trippin'…
yall too old to be actin' like this!

HEAD STAGEHAND
Ladies, come. We need to get started.

Ginni grabs Antoinette by the arm.

GINNI
Come on so we can see what they are
talking about with these envelopes.

All ladies ascend to the stage except Antoinette

ANTOINETTE
Yea you betta walk off!

TONYA
I ain't worried about you!

ANTOINETTE
You should be!

HEAD STAGEHAND
We can't get started unless we are *all* present.

GINNI
Will you come on! Just let it go. I've
got a situation I need to take care of back
home, so the sooner we get started, the
quicker I can get out of here.

*Antoinette ascends to the stage, muttering under
her breath.*

ANTOINETTE
She betta be glad!

TONYA
I don't betta be nothin'!

HEAD STAGEHAND
Ladies… please!

Head Stagehand addresses the entire group.

HEAD STAGEHAND
Now that you are here, I need to find Dr. Simon so we can start our meeting. Why don't you go ahead and take this opportunity to open your envelopes.

Head Stagehand exits stage; all ladies open envelopes and briefly inspects the contents.

TONYA
Greetings ladies, in the name of Our Lord and Savior Jesus **Christ**

ASHLEY
Christ .. On behalf of our generous benefactor, Dr. Daviyana **Simon**….

ANNE
Simon … our organization would like to extend a helping hand to the bearer of this **letter**….

GINNI
letter …provided you are Christian, willingly fornicated and your child is not a result from any type of sexual **assault.**

147

ANTOINETTE

assault …The intention of this letter is to invite you to take part in a life-changing **program**.

TONYA

program …that can provide economic stability for each of your children until they reach the age of 18.

All the women adlib while turning the page; reacting to the good news in character; Ashley calms the group in order to continue reading.

ASHLEY

In order to be awarded financial help for your **children**…

ANNE

children …you must receive the certificate of completion for the mandatory counseling **session**…

TONYA

session …In Dr. Simon's program called "Baby Mama Boot Camp".

Ginni quickly looks up from the letter.

GINNI

Hold up! I am not anybody's baby mama!

Rest of the ladies look up from letter with Ginni's comment.; Anne will join Antoinette's song.

ANTOINETTE

What's wrong with bein' a baby mama? Shoot, Fantasia even got a song about us!…. *B. A. B. Y. M. A. M. A. … this goes out to all my baby mamas….*

GINNI

Girl….you are so ghetto!

TONYA

And triflin' too … just like I said before!

ANTOINETTE

Whateva! Like yall two betta than me. Don't forget all of you was on the Maury Show too.

ASHLEY

Come on, let's just keep reading and see what the rest of the letter says.

GINNI

Here's Dr. Simon's proposition for you, ladies….

ANTOINETTE

If you can make it through Baby Mama Boot Camp…

ANNE

you will be granted a support payment…

TONYA

for each child. until their 18th birthday…

149

ALL LADIES
In the amount of $1000 per month!

Commotion erupts: Anne immediately faints; Ashley drops to her knees crying, thanking Jesus; Ginni nods her head, rubs hands together and shows signs of thinking a plan; Antoinette counts to six with her fingers, rubs her pregnant stomach realizing how much money she will get; Tonya and Antoinette jump around, screaming and yelling- they then hug each other in celebration, realize who they are hugging and break the embrace to continue celebrating individually; they take their seats, adlibbing in character.

HEAD STAGEHAND
So I see that you all have read the contents of the letter.

Affirmative responses by group in character.

HEAD STAGEHAND
Now…you do know that in order to receive the support payments from our organization, you *must* complete this counseling session in order to receive this certificate. (*raises certificates in the air*)

Affirmative responses by group in character;

HEAD STAGEHAND
I must also inform you that any future children conceived out-of-wedlock

beyond today will *not* be covered under the program.

ANNE
Not that I am planning on having any more kids… but why is that?

HEAD STAGEHAND
This is to ensure that some **women** will not continue having more **children** just to obtain more money.

Ladies adlib in character and turn their attention towards Antoinette, who exploits her pregnancy

ANTOINETTE
He said *beyond* today… I'm already pregnant, so dis one counts too, right?

HEAD STAGEHAND
Yes, we will provide for that child as well.

As ladies negatively adlib in character, Antoinette breaks into song.

ANTOINETTE
"Don't need no hateration…"

Ladies continue to adlib in character as Head Stagehand tries to regain control of group.

HEAD STAGEHAND
Lastly, all of you **must** prove your less-than- perfect financial situations

concerning your children are the fault of their less-than- satisfactory fathers.

Ladies continue to adlib in character

ANTOINETTE
Well, I have to admit that Freddie… he was *more* than satisfactory…Not like Sean though.. I had to teach him a few *thangs!*

Antoinette laughs and slaps five with Ginni.

TONYA
And probably gave him a few *thangs* too!

Ladies react in character to the confrontation as Tonya and Antoinette face-off again.

HEAD STAGEHAND
Ladies please,… Let's stay focused! Any display of violence will warrant immediate removal from the program.

Head Stagehand looks toward window as Tonya and Antoinette settle down

HEAD STAGEHAND
I must apologize to you all for the tardiness of Dr. Simon. She is never late, as this is her program…. Well, while we are waiting for her to get here, I will just have to start without her….Oh, yea, before we begin, there is one further thing I need you all to be aware of.

152

TONYA

I knew it!…. Somethin' is up with this!

ASHLEY

It did sound too good to be true.

HEAD STAGEHAND

There is a competition you must participate in at the end in order to awarded the money.

ANNE

What kind of competition you talkin' bout?

HEAD STAGEHAND

We'll cross that bridge when we come to it.

Head Stagehand goes into " drill sergeant" mode.

HEAD STAGEHAND

Welcome to Baby Mama Boot Camp! What happens in this camp stays in this camp! We are here because of your individual choices and to make all of you take a good look at yourselves. As a baby mama, you need to see what your choice is doing to our country!

ANNE

What you mean, we doin' somethin' to our country?

153

ASHLEY
We ain't doin' nothin' to nobody.

ANTOINETTE
We just doin' us!

TONYA
Nah…we doin' us… Nasty Girl, you doin' a whole bunch of people!

Antoinette stands up while Tonya motions for Head Stagehand to remove Antoinette from group;

HEAD STAGEHAND
Ladies….

GINNI
Sit down Antoinette! Can't you see she is just trying get you upset? Don't forget about the money!

Antoinette sits down, staring at Tonya.

ASHLEY
Excuse me… but didn't **both** of you test the same man for paternity.

GINNI
Now, *that* is nasty!

HEAD STAGEHAND
Excuse me…Ladies!

ANNE
Yall do know that by being with the same man she *doin'*, you *doin'* a whole bunch of people too!

GINNI
Look at the kettle calling the skillet black.. Mrs. Home Wrecker!

ANNE
What about you... Ms. Church Wrecker!

HEAD STAGEHAND
Ladies!!!

ANTOINETTE
All of yall you need to be worryin' bout yo' own selves!

TONYA
Nah.. *you* need to worrin' about finding the father of your other twin! Or will it take another 6 shows to find that one!

ANNE
I know that's right!

ANTOINETTE
I know you not talkin'! Don't forget you the one that likes to keep the money in the family... Uncle ... Nephew... Nasty!

ANNE
I did what I had to do... I needed the money...

Yana enters stage-right during commotion dressed in Army gear.

YANA
BABY...MAMA...MANIA!

Ginni stands up immediately.

GINNI
Excuse me!... What are *you* doing here?

YANA
I belong here.

GINNI
No.... No you don't! This meeting is for single mothers...

HEAD STAGEHAND
Baby mamas!

GINNI
Whatever... either way, you don't qualify to be here because you can't have kids.

YANA
I am more than qualified to be here.

HEAD STAGEHAND
Dr .Simon has finally arrived everyone!

Ginni looks around to see if another person is entering the room.

GINNI
Where is this Dr. Simon you brought

156

along with you? I need tell her about herself and her so-called baby mama boot camp.

YANA
Go ahead, I'm right here.

GINNI
But your name is Yana …

YANA
Daviyana Simon is the name my mama gave me.

ANNE
Hey, that's the lady you was backstage with…

TONYA
Ooooh… so that's the Pastor's wife?

ASHLEY
She the one who had a baby by her pastor?

ANTOINETTE
Her pastor who is also her ex-husband! (*starts singing*) *These are my confessions…*

YANA
(*Looking at Ginni*) Please forgive my tardiness ladies. I had to deal with my own issues before I could help you deal with yours….

Ginni muttering, returns to her seat.

GINNI
And who you supposed to be anyway… Some broke-down G.I. Jane?

HEAD STAGEHAND

You will address Master Sergeant Simon
with respect! ....And that goes for all of
you! Your behaviors are the reason why
she is even here, trying to help you!

YANA addresses each woman.

YANA

I got this! ...I am here because of you
Tonya ... you that pressed for some man
that you beg him to be with you...then
you keep having babies by him.. the
same man that is marrying someone
else?

Tonya adlibs remorsefully to Yana's comment.

YANA

I am here because of you Ginni...
sleeping with a married man who
happens to also be your *Pastor*... I guess
no man is off limits to you!

Ginni adlibs smugly to Yana's comment.

YANA

Antoinette, Antoinette.. Antoinette...
Just for the simple fact that your twins
have different fathers indicates you
really need Baby Mama Boot Camp!

*Antoinette adlibs in Ghetto-fabulous style to
Yana's comment.*

YANA
Ashley… I going to come back to you

Yana addresses Anne who is noticeably quiet.

YANA
I am here because of you Anne… just destroyed a family when you slept with your husband's own nephew... look what happens when people get what they pay for!....(*turns attention to Ashley*) Ashley, how old are you?

ASHLEY
Almost 18**....**

YANA
Look, for the rest of these women here, it may be too late for them to change… but your age group represents those at most risk for contracting diseases…

TONYA
Excuse me…change is never too late for *any* of us… all things are possible to them that believe!

HEAD STAGEHAND
Amen, Sista! We serve a God who sits high and looks low. We just have to believe!

ASHLEY
Well, I believed Malik when he said he loved me.

ANNE

Baby girl , they always say they love you.

ASHLEY

And he said he wanted to marry me too!

TONYA

I bet he said you were his fiancé, right?

ASHLEY

Uh huh… yea…

ANTOINETTE

Where da ring at?

GINNI

Ladies…. Ladies…ladies…. 40 might be the new 20, but a friend with benefits and no ring… that's **not** the new fiancé!

Yana shakes her head in dismay while looking at Head Stagehand.

YANA

Babymamamania!

GINNI

Hey Rambo, where did you come up with this *Baby… mama… mania*?

Yana reaches for one of the books from the stack on the desk and holds it up before the group.

YANA

Actually it is the name of this book I have used to develop this special program that addresses the very issues before you now….

ASHLEY

But what does "Babymamamania" actually mean?

HEAD STAGEHAND

Well, it is derived from the word **baby mama -**a mother who is not married to or living with her child's father and **mania-** an out-of-control and widespread trend.

ANTOINETTE

But I thought a baby mama was any single mother.

YANA

Not true, because many single mothers were actually married *before* their circumstances changed. Matter of fact, one definition of *Babymamamania* deals with what you all were just discussing – It is the pop-culture trend of baby mamas referring to her baby daddy as a fiancé when there is neither commitment nor engagement ring in sight!

TONYA

But while they be "lovin'" you, they be sayin' that they *want* to be with you…

ANTOINETTE

Talkin' bout how that they want you to give dem babies, like it's a badge of honor or somthin'..

ASHLEY

They be lyin' when they say how they gonna be there for you and the kids!

YANA

See what I mean....*Babymamamania* - The widespread fallacy that if a man continues to have relations on a regular basis with his baby mama he must still have feelings for her... Not! Don't confuse mere convenience with caring... you probably were just the only warm body he could come up with at the moment!

HEAD STAGEHAND

I am sure most of you baby mamas have learned the hard way that a man will tell you anything you want to hear to get from you everything that you are willing to give him.

Ladies respond with affirmation of the statement in character.

GINNI

Look, let's get it straight right now; I am *not* a baby mama! I am a single parent!

HEAD STAGEHAND
Do you think calling yourself a single parent changes the fact that you really are a baby mama?

GINNI
You don't know me, you can't talk to me like that! No amount of money is worth me being disrespected by a Dr. Phil wanna-be.

Head Stagehand approaches Ginni, in her face.

HEAD STAGEHAND
Just so you know... I am going to talk to you in the manner in which you need to hear what I have to say. And if you don't like it, you can leave!

Rest of the group laughs and jesters at Ginni

YANA
And that goes for the *rest* of you baby mamas too!

Group instantly stops laughing as Ginni laughs at them in turn.

GINNI
Well, *just so you know*, I will never consider myself a baby mama, no matter what you say.... I am a single lady... I make my own money... I have my own place... And *I know* that I will never have to lower myself to sell my body to

take care of my child like some of these Ghetto Hoodrats do. I would never choose to use my body like that!

Mood in the group becomes tense as the women reflect on their pasts; Anne responds in anger.

ANNE
Well maybe you didn't always *have* a choice of what even happens to your own body...or over what they did to it! You ever think about that?

Antoinette finds it difficult to share.

ANTOINETTE
Yea sometimes the.... "*stuff*" ... that they do to your body when you little makes you want it... makes you crave it even more when you get grown.....

Ashley is on the verge of tears, fighting them back as best as she can.

ASHLEY
Or maybe they done so much to you back then that you hate yourself, so you even don't care what they do to your body now.

HEAD STAGEHAND
Ladies, no matter what has transpired in your pasts, you cannot let it control your destiny! You may not have had a choice when you were young, but selling your

164

body in order to care for your children should never be an option!

ANNE
You don't know nothin' about our lives!

YANA
Well, I know you are all professing to be Christians! So, no woman who trusts God should ever have to resort to such measures!

ANNE
What does me being a Christian got to do with anything?

YANA
Your Christian walk has to do with everything! Let me ask you a question…Do you think God's anointing is in that bed with you when your sales transaction is underway?

ANTOINETTE
You ain't gotta be like that! Just because you got some big job don't mean you can look down on us if we gotta do what we gotta do!

HEAD STAGEHAND
That's not a choice you as a Christian woman should ever make. Your Father is rich! He owns cattle on a thousand hills!

TONYA

Yall don't know how hard life can be! You can't possibly understand the choices *they* had to make sometimes.

ANNE

How can God forgive all our mess? I know this might make Him mad... but sometimes I think if I don't do it... If I don't go ahead and sell my body, how else am I'm gonna be able to make it as a single mother!

YANA

No, you don't understand! Before you all start making assumptions about me not knowing what you have gone through, you need to check yourselves! I know what its is like to be raised by a single mother... She would say to us "God promises His children food, shelter and clothing, and He promises to keeps his promise!" Oh, I understand... I watched my mother drag herself from one job to the next to make sure all of us kids had groceries from Shoppers on our table, Wal-Mart clothes on our backs and Payless Shoes on our feet! I am blessed to tell you that my mother never sold her soul or her body to take care of us! If anything, she worked herself into an early grave so that I could have this very opportunity to be before all of you today. So, don't tell me as single mother you can't make it!

YANA calms from the climatic finish to speech; sounding a bit defeated.

YANA

Look, I'm sure I am basically wasting my breath. The truth is that most of you *Christians* are not even bothered about having relations outside the sanctity of marriage; that's the biggest shame of all... Nonetheless, we need to finish the last portion of Baby Mama Boot camp and that's the competition for the money.

Ladies liven up, interest returns because of the money.

HEAD STAGEHAND

You all are going to play a special game of Simon Says and whoever is left standing, will leave with the first month's $1000 payment per child today!

All women react enthusiastically in character to the news, especially Antoinette who would leave with $7000.

HEAD STAGEHAND

Also, as an added bonus, all winners of the competition will split a cash prize of $100,000!

Group goes wild; Antoinette is visibly trying to figure the mathematics then tries to calm group.

ANTOINETTE
So, if there is only one winner, she gets the whole hun'ed thou, right?

HEAD STAGEHAND
That's correct!

Group adlibs at prospect of winning and taking home additional $100,000.

YANA
Now, I need all of you to line up across the floor… stretch your arms out so you can have some room.

Ladies adlibbing in character line up quickly across the stage.

YANA
Remember whoever is still standing at the end of the game, will win the money….. Ready?...Here we go… Simon Says, if Christ Jesus died to redeem you from your sin, take one step forward.

All ladies step forward, happily commenting on their relationship with Jesus; Yana walks around group as like a drill Sergeant.

YANA
So, why are you Christians fornicating! Last time I checked, that was a major sin! What kind of witness for salvation do you have when you are underneath a

man who is not your husband!.... Simon Says straighten up!

Ladies straighten up quickly.

HEAD STAGEHAND
You Christians are supposed to be the light to a dying world by living in Victory Over Wickedness! Umph, umph umph....

YANA
Simon Says extend your left arm forward, palm down.

Ladies struggle with the command.

YANA
Bring your left palm to your left eye.

Ladies do not move as Tonya adlibs about "Left-Eye" from TLC.

ANTOINETTE
(Starts singing) I don't want no scrubs...

YANA
Ladies, you need to stay focused through this competition... Simon Says bring your left palm to your left eye.

All ladies complete the task.

HEAD STAGEHAND

This is what you are supposed to be ladies...Strong soldiers in the Lord's Army! How do you expect to be more than a conqueror if you don't put on ...

Head Stagehand says one item to each individual lady, acting out the description of list

HEAD STAGEHAND

-The helmet of salvation...

-The breastplate of righteousness...

-The belt of truth buckled around your waist...

-The shield of faith, to extinguish the flaming arrows of the evil one ....

-The sword of the Spirit, which is the word of God.

YANA

Simon Says if you are proud to be a single lady.., emancipated..., got your stuff together, put your left hand up in the air...

Ladies complete the task in character. As following song breaks out, ladies join in on dance in order below.

ANTOINETTE
All the single ladies... all the single ladies...

ANNE & ASHLEY
All the single ladies... all the single ladies...

TONYA & GINNI
Put your hands ups, oh oh oh... etc

Yana joins in on the dance as Head Stagehand shakes his head.

ALL LADIES
If you liked it, then you should'a put a ring on it etc...

HEAD STAGEHAND
Hello.... We *are* playing a game of Simon Says here...

YANA and Ladies regain composure in character, putting left hands back in air;

YANA
Simon Says go ahead ladies and drop your arm!

Ladies complete the task as Yana and Head Stagehand pace around group.

HEAD STAGEHAND
We want you to see how God views today's single lady. In the Bible, you will only find four categories of women

based on their sexuality. Here is where today's single lady fits....

YANA
Simon Says if you are a virgin, take a step back.

None of the ladies move.

ANTOINETTE
Well, ain't none of us movin' on this one!

Ladies adlib in character to remark.

YANA
The *virgins* in the bible knew no man... Simon Says if you are a faithful wife, take a step back.

None of the ladies move.

TONYA
We *all* know neither of yall desperate house*wives can* move on this one either!
Ladies adlib in character to remark.

YANA
The virtuous *wife* in the bible only knew her husband... Simon Says if you are a widow, take a step back.

None of the ladies move.

ASHLEY

Antoinette, you might as well go ahead
and step back, cuz you 'bout killed yo
husband on that stage out there with all
those people watching him found out the
twins got different daddies!

Ladies adlib in character to remark.

YANA

The Godly *widow* with children
generally knew no other man... Simon
Says if you are a harlot, take a step back.

*Ladies respond negatively and loudly to being
called a harlot. None of the ladies move.*

YANA

And then there's the *harlot*; she knew
everybody else! So let me ask the
question again... Simon Says, if your
activities as a single lady can only fall
into the fourth category of harlot, take..
a...step...back!

*All ladies reluctantly step back, adlibbing in
character, under their breath.*

YANA

There you go! It is what it is!... Simon
Says if you have never been married put
your left hand on top your head.

Tonya and Ashley complete the task.

YANA

You two represent the one third of all custodial mothers that have never been married. God himself created marriage! How dare you cast that notion aside by having babies out of wedlock, like it doesn't matter or won't have any dire consequences! ...Go ahead, put your hand down.

Tonya drops her arm and reacts about losing while other ladies respond in character; Tonya returns to her chair in character. Yana addresses Ashley.

YANA

Simon Says, put your hand down.

Ashley completes the task as Yana turns her attention back to the remaining ladies that are still standing.

YANA

Simon Says if you have a court order for child support, raise one arm in the air.

TONYA

Well, I love Sean too much to get the "man" involved in our finances...

ANNE

I bet he don't give you no money on his own, do he?.... See... I don't have to worry about goin' to court, cause' my husband pays *very* well...

ASHLEY

Yea, we know… we heard him cryin' from the Green Room…

Ginni addresses Yana with spite.

GINNI

As for me, you **and** Pastor should be getting your child support papers in the mail by the end of the week!

ANTOINETTE

But what if I don't have a court order for all of 'em?.

HEAD STAGEHAND

Do you have a court order for at least one of them?

Antoinette completes the task.

YANA

Do you all know more than 40% of all custodial parents do not have court-ordered child support …..I wonder how many women *can't* even receive child support because they *can't* establish paternity! Pathetic! Simon says raise both arms in the air if you don't know who the fathers of your children are!

Antoinette looks at the other women as she is the only one to raise both arms; other ladies adlib.

YANA

You ought to be ashamed of yourself!
Put your arms down!

*Antoinette thinks it's a trick to get her to lose the
Simon Says game; she laughs a bit.*

ANTOINETTE

Nah… you not gonna get me out… uh uh. No
"Srrrr" I know how to play dis here game.

Head Stagehand circles around Antoinette.

HEAD STAGEHAND

Look, do yourself a favor, don't make
the seventh trip to the Maury show,
because you make yourself look like boo
boo the fool. It's already one thing that
you don't even know who the father is,
but then to go on national TV and put
your loose life on display, *Ms. Christian.*
What kind of Godly witness are you to
the nation. Even worse, what kind of
witness are you on behalf of all of us
Black people… don't you know what
one sees in some black people, they
believe for the whole race?

*Antoinette starts to show signs of arms beginning
to hurt from being raised over her head; Head
Stagehand addresses Antoinette in "Martin
Luther King" tone.*

176

HEAD STAGEHAND

But in your case, all of America.... *all of God's children, black men and white men, Jews and Gentiles, Protestants and Catholics, will be able to join hands* and *sing in the words of the "new" Negro Spiritual ... find the babydaddy at last, find the babydaddy at last. Thank God Almighty, you found the babydaddy at last!*

YANA

Simon Says put your arms down!

Antoinette puts visibly sore arms down, Ginni speaks to Antoinette; not paying attention.

GINNI

Girl, I am glad they said something to you about going back on the Maury Show...

YANA

If you are Black, step forward!

Ginni steps forward, not paying attention.
GINNI

Please don't make us look bad any more.

Ginni realizes that she has lost and all respond in character; Ginni returns to her seat, sulking.

YANA

Simon Says if you are Black, step forward.

All Black ladies step forward.

YANA
Do you know that Black Americans represent only 12 percent of the total U.S. population, but make up more than 70 percent of all gonorrhea cases?

Ladies react in character to the statistics as Head Stagehand moves behind the group, stating each fact one by one.

HEAD STAGEHAND
Did you also know that 44% of those living with AIDS in the USA are *Black*.

Ladies react in character.

HEAD STAGEHAND
40% of Americans who died last year from AIDS were *Black*.

Ladies react in character.

HEAD STAGEHAND
51% of all *new* AIDS cases last year were *Black*.

Ladies react in character more vocal than previous, disturbed by the data.

YANA
"Black Mother", put your right hand over your heart.

Anne, not paying attention, is out of the game; Ladies adlib in character.

YANA

Simon says, "Black Mother", put your right hand over your heart.

Ashley & Antoinette complete task, adlibbing in character

YANA

All Black mothers need to know this… 63% of children under the age of 13 diagnosed with HIV/AIDS are Black.

All ladies solemnly comment in character .

YANA

Simon Says if you are between the ages of 15 and 24, put your hand down to your side.

Ashley and Antoinette complete task.

YANA

Simon Says if you are from Texas, Louisiana, Mississippi, Alabama, Georgia or South Carolina, take two steps forward.

Ashley and Antoinette complete the task.

YANA

You two represent whom the Center for Disease Control finds as the most dangerous person in the United States of America to be intimate with!

Ladies demeanors change as Head Stagehand barks the accusation.

HEAD STAGEHAND
Who is this menace to society?... She is Black.. She is between the ages of 15 and 24... and she lives within the area of our county reporting the highest cases of Chlamydia and Gonorrhea.... that's the dirty south!

Ashley and Antoinette react in character.

YANA
By the way, are either of you from Mississippi?

Ashley speaks up, voice quivering.

ASHLEY
I'm is.

HEAD STAGEHAND
Mississippi, just so you know, leads the pack within the Dirty Dirty.

Both ladies drop their head in shame. Ashley is convicted to tears; Yana barks at the pair.

YANA
Oh, my God! The two of you actually need to save our country from *yourselves*! If neither of you repent for your sin...If you refuse to contain your lustful ways... you will continue to put our nation at risk!

Ashley is crying uncontrollably, Antoinette wipes tears from her eyes with her shoulders.

YANA
Sit your wicked selves down!

Ashley takes one step toward chairs and collapses in hysterical tears while Antoinette moves toward chairs and realizes that she has lost the game, adlibbing in character.

HEAD STAGEHAND
Game over!

Ladies react to the broken Ashley in character as Yana approaches and soothes her.

YANA
Give him your life, daughter! Jesus died for your sin… He wants to give you life more abundantly.

Yana wipes tears from Ashley's eyes and then addresses group.

YANA
Look, how about if I have my assistant give you ladies a second chance at the money?

GINNI
I personally don't need you to do anything for me. I've already taken every thing from you anyway!

Yana takes a deep breath, looking upward and ignores Ginni.

ASHLEY

I don't care about the game or the money anymore; I just want to live right.

ANTOINETTE

Well, I care about the money… can you finish tellin' us about the second chance?

Yana reaches over to grab a book and a T-shirt , handing both to Anne.

YANA

All you have to do is accept this gift from our ministry to help you control you own Babymamamania…. play one more round of Simon Says and then answer one simple question with a "yes" and the money can be yours.

Ladies adlib in character as they get up for book and shirt, with Ginni being last.

YANA

Ladies, can you please put your T-Shirts on….

Ladies adlib in character as they put on t-shirts

TONYA

Hey, what does the **V.O.W** stand for?

YANA

Victory **O**ver **W**ickedness. This is how God expects you to live… this why Jesus gave His life in the first place! Come on ladies, place your gifts on your seat and stand up in line again.

Ladies begin to re-from the single line excitedly, except Anne who has to be persuaded by Yana to rejoin the game

HEAD STAGEHAND

And while you ladies are standing, remember what the Bible tells us....when you think you can't stand any longer .... After you have done everything you can to stand... keep standing!

YANA

That's right ladies... keep standing... Look, I am even going to help you all out and let you know ahead of time that the Simon Says move has two parts.

Ladies respond with excitement for the tip as Head Stagehand continues the game.

HEAD STAGEHAND

Simon Says... put your right hand over your heart to make a **V.O.W** to live in victory *and* cross your right leg over your left.

Ladies carefully complete the task and show enthusiasm for progressing; Head Stagehand breaks into a preaching "tune".

HEAD STAGEHAND

Now, when you ladies can answer the question with a yes.. **huh**!

Ladies responds as if listening to a minister in church..

HEAD STAGEHAND

You will find… **huh**!...where the true fault lies…huh!

…you will find who really.. **huh**! … is to blame for your financial situation…

…you will learn …**huh**… how your child could have been spared … huh..

spared from dead-beat from fathers that didn't want them…. **huh**!…

Ladies adlib agreeing strongly on the dead beat dad verbiage

HEAD STAGEHAND

…Spared from fathers that never really wanted their mothers either …. huh!

Ladies abruptly become silent with previous comment.

HEAD STAGEHAND

….They **could'a** been spared from the hurt…, huh!

Ladies get involved with preaching as if in church.

HEAD STAGEHAND

….They **would'a** been spared from the pain… huh!….Those precious children ***should'a*** been spared from all their agony and shame ….

Head Stagehand is overcome in praise.

HEAD STAGEHAND
G.P. are you with me!

ALL LADIES except Ginni
Oh yeah, me and the church ain't goin' no where!

HEAD STAGEHAND
G.P. are you with me!

ALL LADIES except Ginni
Oh yeah, me and the church ain't goin' no where!

HEAD STAGEHAND
I promise the Stomp… *(Lean ear toward audience to have them finish the song)* the whole stomp, nothin but the stomp…

HEAD STAGEHAND
It ain't over, it ain't over!

GINNI
Will you all just come on and get to the point!!!!

All ladies and Head Stagehand abruptly calm down from the "spirit", then picks of stack of certificates in hand.

YANA
Now remember ladies, all you have to do is answer my question with a "yes", and the money is yours! And since somebody can't get with the tune… let me finish up in a poetic fashion…..

If you ladies had vowed to live holy, to live right, and if you had kept your legs crossed tight?

185

*Here's the very question you
ladies must face.. Would there
even be a baby in the first place!?!*

HEAD STAGEHAND
NO "Sirrr" (*tears the certificates in half*)

YANA
So ladies, take a look at yourselves and
see who really is a fault here.

*Ladies adlib in character concerning the
revelation concerning their behaviors as
Antoinette uncrosses her legs and removes a
pillow from under her shirt.*

ANTOINETTE
Well, I guess I don't have to pretend I'm
pregnant no more!

*Antoinette tosses pillow down and exits with Ladies
following behind her, adlibbing about her deception*
as *Head Stagehand and Yana begin to stack up
chairs etc. When all the ladies have exited, Head
Stagehand retrieves pillow .*

HEAD STAGEHAND
Just when I thought I had seen it all…

Head Stagehand tosses pillow to Yana.

YANA
That's a new one on me too. I don't
think we have ever had someone fake a
pregnancy in one of our sessions!

*Antoinette re-enters unbeknownst to Yana and
Head Stagehand.*

HEAD STAGEHAND

I feel so sorry for her husband. I don't think he can handle much more from that woman of his.

YANA

Perhaps you should keep this to yourself or those Stage Managers will want them back for a show about secrets.

Antoinette rushes back to snatch the pillow from Yana's grasp.

ANTOINETTE

Gimme dis…. I might need this later!

Antoinette puts pillow under her arm, exiting while adlibbing about the conversation she overheard; Yana and Head Stagehand

END ACT 2

END PLAY

Curtain Call

"Man in the Mirror" by Michael Jackson
plays through curtain call

~~~~~~~~~~~~~~~~~~~~~~~~~~~~~~

Stagehands

Lip Sync/Dancers

Diane & C.K.Sha'

Sean, Daryl, Malik and Matthew

Margarita & Bridgett

Stage Manager #1 & #2

Head Stagehand & Yana

Anne, Ashley Antoinette, Ginni and Tonya

Director

~~~~~~~~~~~~~~~~~~~~~~~~~~~~~~